IN THE
MEANTIME

LESSONS AND LEARNING
FROM A CAREER IN BEER

NICK MILLER

In the Meantime
ISBN 978-1-912300-92-1 (paperback)
ISBN 978-1-912300-98-3 (hardback)
eISBN 978-1-912300-93-8

Published in 2022 by Right Book Press
Printed in the UK

Contents

To my family and all aspiring business people whatever they make, sell or serve.

Introduction

I used to collect beer mats when I was a boy. Growing up in a small village near Burton-on-Trent in the 70s, I'd catch the aroma of hops and sulphur in the back of my throat on a Saturday morning when I rode my bike to get a bacon sandwich from Nick's Café – the 'Burton snatch', they called that smell. The town may not have been the powerhouse it had been in the 19th century, when it accounted for a quarter of Britain's beer production, but it was still clearly a beer town that my dad moved us to when he was sent by the British Tyre and Rubber Company (BTR) to set up their new factory. Dad was an engineer, analytical and precise, scientific in his knowledge of rubber production processes; Mum was gregarious, a popular teacher and a stalwart of the local amateur dramatics society. We lived in Marchington, a village of no more than a thousand people just outside Burton, and I went to school in Uttoxeter.

This was the land of Bass, Marstons, Ind Coope, where they brewed beer made from the kind of hard Burton water

7

which gave it such a distinctive, hoppy flavour. Later on, I would discover that the industry phrase 'Burtonising the water' was shorthand for the process of adding calcium sulphate and bicarbonates to mimic that kind of hard, dry water which showed off the sweet flavour of the hops. In the winter, there was so much steam coming off the Burton breweries that they formed clouds which produced hoppy-smelling snow. I didn't know about all that as a lad of ten cycling around the Staffordshire lanes, getting into trouble, talking my way out of it. I don't really know why I started collecting beer mats, sticking them up on the wall of my bedroom. Drawn to it, I suppose.

We moved to Hanbury, a smaller village than Marchington, after Dad was made redundant by BTR. By the time I was 12, my mates and I had befriended a lovely couple, Ron and Min, who ran the Cock Inn in the village and we'd hang about playing pool in the back room and getting a taste of very watered-down shandy. As the months went by, either Ron or Min would slowly increase the beer proportion so that by the time I was 14, I knew how to drink a pint. They were great days: I bought an old Honda 'Grandad' motorbike for £20 and my mates fixed it up for me so that I could drive illegally over to my lifelong mate Mike Fenwick's house. Forty years later and Mike now entertains his kids with stories about old Miller swerving up to his house on an illegal knackered motorbike. I played basketball for the school but always got sent off because you were only allowed five fouls. I got into the football first team, covering up an innate lack of talent with an excess of energy. I was playing pretty serious cricket too, learning how to apply myself to that magnificent game. I was outdoors all the time, knocking about in Hanbury with mates like Dicko, Tiny, Bruce and Welly, smoking cigarettes behind barn walls and making up stories about how tough we were or which of the two village girls fancied us the most. Trying to make me study was painful, and I'd make a cursory attempt at doing my homework late in the evening with the John Peel show playing punk music in the background.

When I was 13, Dad left. The redundancy had hit him hard and as quite an introverted, methodical man, maybe he had found himself living in the shadow of his popular, glamorous wife. I don't know and I've never really wanted to find out what went on; there's always two sides to every story and I've never been that interested in knowing either. Dad moved out and for the first few months would visit occasionally at weekends. One Saturday he appeared and told me he was taking me and my younger brother, Peter, to see Nottingham Forest play Chelsea at home. Even at 13, I knew that was a bad idea. He told us he was going to buy tickets at the ground.

'Dad, you won't be able to. You don't know what these grounds are like. We won't be able to get in.'

He'd have none of it. We got to City Ground and of course there was a pitched battle going on outside the gates between the hard nut supporters of both teams, blokes smashing merry hell out of each other with bicycle chains and clubs, police pelted with bottles. This was what football was like in the 70s. Inevitably we couldn't even get close to the ticket office – in fact, it was madness taking two young lads anywhere near such carnage. As we drove back, I shouted at him for the first and only time in my life, all my frustration and hurt maybe coming out with plenty of implied support for my mum. And that was it. He dropped us off, and never came back. I never saw him again for the rest of his life.

Looking back, I suppose my parents' divorce granted me the independence I'd sort of already claimed. Dad's departure left a permanent mark: for a long time, maybe for the rest of my life, I oscillated from thinking 'Damn you', to feeling driven somehow to make him proud of me, even in his absence. Mum as a single parent found it quite challenging for the first year or two, and while I was still 15 she took Peter off to stay with her best friend in Guernsey for a few weeks, leaving me on my own in the house in Hanbury. She left me a hundred quid to buy myself food and said there were some tins in the cupboard if I got hungry. When she finally came back, she looked in the cupboard and found it was empty.

'You've eaten all the tins,' she said. 'What did you spend that hundred quid on? It wasn't food, was it?'

She was right, of course. For those few weeks, I fed myself with the tins, eating delights like stuffing on toast, and I spent the money on beer and cigarettes. And of course, I had a party. The only way Mum found out that I'd had a party was when she discovered cigarette ash underneath the toilet seat. She spotted that the day after she got back, and she came into the kitchen where I was frying myself an egg.

'You've had a party, haven't you?' she demanded, coming right up to me.

'How do you know that?' I stammered.

'I just know,' she said.

So I said, 'Well? So what?'

And she replied, 'Were there girls here?'

'Maybe.'

'Let me give you some advice,' she said. 'One: be nice. Two: wear a condom. Three: no underage. 4. Never show off to your mates. 5. Leave them satisfied.' This is advice which I have subsequently passed on to all the young men in my own family, hopefully with grandsons to come.

And with that, she walked out of the kitchen. Looking back now, I can see how she had to be the mum and the dad for both me and Peter, and she did a bloody good job of it. We were a handful, Peter and I, always scrapping, always getting into scrapes. Once, I remember our school maths teacher coming round to the house for some supper with Mum, and Peter had sneakily been drinking cider with his mates. He staggered up to his bedroom feeling very unwell but couldn't hold it all in, and managed to get his window up in time to throw up out of it. Unfortunately, all over the maths teacher's car down below. When the teacher came out to head off home, he took one look at his car.

'My, Mrs Miller,' he said. 'The birds around here make a right old mess, don't they?'

By this time I was doubled up with laughter, but Mum charged upstairs, found the culprit and hauled him down to clean the teacher's car before he went home.

Mum's no different to this day. She lives in a retirement village now not far from me with her second husband Mike, a very good man whom she married ten years after Dad left. She's still the life and soul of the party, running the village croquet club, organising canasta evenings. Me? I'm 57, living on the south coast with my wife Em, my three kids all grown up and making their way in the world. And it seems to me now that life is a magical process like the brewing of beer, an alchemy of ingredients, application, special moments, patience, endurance. You get lucky sometimes in life, and any brewer will tell you that luck can play a part in the discovery of a new beer flavour, but it's about other things too: persistence, listening, learning, striving, sharing.

In 2015 I was the chief executive of a relatively niche but highly successful craft beer business called Meantime. Located in Greenwich, south-east London, it was the brainchild of a brilliant brewer called Alastair Hook, who had formed the business at the turn of the millennium. Alastair had achieved great things, had made some truly outstanding beer, but by 2011 both he and his shareholders knew that change was needed. The business was leaking cash, it wasn't expanding and it was struggling to fulfil the limited orders it was getting from the on- and off-trade.[1] After a 25-year career in the corporate beer industry, working for the traditional British brewer Bass plc and the global drinks giant SAB Miller, I decided to take the plunge and leave the 'slippery pole' of corporate life to join this rebellious little craft beer company as its chief executive. In just four years, with the support of a truly fantastic team of people, we turned it round and sold it to SAB Miller. A wide spread of people, both shareholders and employees, shared in the proceeds of that deal; in purely selfish terms, it enabled me and my wife Em to spend a bit more time with Minnie, our spaniel puppy, watching the waves on the south coast.

In the Meantime is the story of those four years, how we turned Meantime Beer into one of the most successful craft

---

1 In the alcohol industry, the 'on-trade' covers all the venues where consumers can buy and consume alcohol on the premises: pubs, bars, clubs, restaurants. The 'off-trade' is made up of retail businesses where consumers can buy alcohol to take away: off licences, supermarkets, corner shops, cash and carry businesses.

beers this country has ever seen, and how we negotiated a sale which shocked the entire industry. It is, primarily, a practical guide whose lessons, I hope, can be usefully used by those aiming to make a success in business, whether in beer or bananas. But it's also going to be informed by my own story. I want to show how a successful business strategy and execution, like the turnaround and sale of Meantime Beer, is really the result of a lifetime's learning and experience and the people that you meet and with whom you work along the way. When you're busy doing something as a 10-year-old, a 20-year-old, a 30-year-old, 'in the meantime' other less tangible processes are going on in the background of your life. You're developing, just like that gorgeous liquid does as it ferments in the brewmaster's beloved tanks.

So while I'll talk in detail about the four Meantime years and how we delivered on our plans, what we all learned from that adventure and what different ingredients went into the success which we shared, at the same time I'll go back over the career I've enjoyed in the beer industry, trying to pick out those elements, stories and people which have contributed to my own memory box of learning. I've found that most of the time when you are benefiting from the influence of a great boss or developing from a unique experience, you're not fully aware of the impact. Often it's only much later that you realise just how much that person or that moment meant to you and to your development.

The success which my Meantime colleagues and I all managed to achieve with the momentous sale of the business came down to the way we all worked together, each of our characters providing a different element to the mix, sharing our experience, knowledge and skills. I was lucky to be the fellow conducting the process. There's a magic about brewing that you taste when you bring that chilled glass to your lips for the first time and let the aromas come off the head. Every brewer knows how difficult, how complicated but also how intensely satisfying it is to manage the process and the ingredients so well that you allow consumers to taste some of that magic. I know full well that I'd been brewed for this moment by a long, arduous and very happy career in an industry I still love.

Success in a consumer-facing business depends on the careful assessment of all the ingredients at your disposal: what you understand of enterprise thinking, teamwork, energy, listening, risk assessment, empathy, strategy, consumer focus. It took me until my mid-40s to know that my own personal ingredients were ready to be applied in a genuinely entrepreneurial situation, and that's the story I'd like to tell you.

This is a practical, how-to book about building a business career as both an intrapreneur and an entrepreneur.[2] It's the perspective of one person who didn't start out with much and who learned how to make the most of experience and the lessons provided by colleagues. I've tried to distil the lessons I've learned over 30 years in the beer business working both within major corporations and at the helm of a small but very successful craft beer company. I'm hoping

---

2 The *Cambridge Dictionary* defines an 'intrapreneur' as 'an employee within a large company who takes direct responsibility for turning an idea into a profitable new product, service, business, etc., often instead of leaving to start their own company. An intrapreneur brings entrepreneurial thinking and skills to building a career path within the structure of an existing organisation.' It defines an 'entrepreneur' as 'someone who starts their own business, especially when this involves seeing a new opportunity'.

that some of what I've experienced will be of assistance to you, the reader, whether you're planning to build your career within a corporate structure or whether you have ambitions to set out on your own. I've tried to set down lessons in as non-preachy a way as possible about how to market and sell a consumer product like beer; I've also offered advice on how to manage your own path, how to work on yourself as a brand-in-progress, based on my own career path with all of its highs and lows. Perhaps it seems obvious, but if you find something that you love doing, then you're probably going to have a much greater chance of being successful. Above all, I've tried to emphasise the absolute importance of never giving up.

Leadership is not a popularity contest; it's about providing the clarity and the consistency that your team needs in order to allow them to perform at their best. In enterprise management terms, it's also about knowing how to behave, learning how to grow as an individual as your organisation grows, understanding how your responsibilities will only grow as the business develops.

If this book helps you to make sense of some of your own business ambitions and to clarify your own business strategy, or to reflect on the skills you may have picked up in your own meantime, then I've done my job. Whether you're thinking about being a brewer yourself, or you're thinking about how to approach an entirely different product or service, I'm with you. I'd like to share with you what I learned along the way and when we get to the end, I'll raise my glass to you and wish you every success in the world.

Chapter One

Taking the Plunge

On Monday 12 September 2011, I walked into the Meantime Brewery in Greenwich on my first day as the chief executive. I was fizzing with energy, even more than usual. I'd spent 25 years in the beer industry, the last five running Miller Brands UK on behalf of the world's biggest beer conglomerate, SAB Miller.[3] I'd achieved some major milestones: at Miller Brands, we'd made Peroni Nastro Azzurro the UK's bestselling premium lager by value, and in many instances changed the way consumers felt about drinking lager – we set up Peroni as a gender-neutral drink for men and women. As a young man at Bass, I'd been made salesman of the year twice in a row. All my working life had been spent inside huge corporations, diligently working my way up through one management role after another and all

---

3 Before it was acquired by Anheauser-Busch InBev (ABI), SAB Miller was the world's second largest brewing group. Originally formed as South African Breweries in 1895, it listed on the London stock market in 1999 and then acquired American brewer Miller Brewing in 2002.

my colleagues up until this moment had been a part of that same corporate landscape.

Now here I was pushing open the door of the only office in the Meantime brewery on Blackhall Lane, a sparsely decorated first-floor room above the brewery tanks on the ground floor, with strip lights, broken Venetian blinds and a few cheap MDF desks scattered about with paper all over them. Thoughtfully, someone had set up a table, which looked more like a wallpaper-pasting trestle, for me to use as a desk. The desks were for master brewer Alastair Hook; Alastair's co-founder and, until my arrival, chief operating officer Ben Joseph; the head brewer at the time, an ebullient American craft brewer called Steve Schmidt; and Lisa Stock, the stalwart and effective invoice and payments manager whose tight and expert credit control did so much to contribute towards our cash flow. Snoozing on blankets in the corner were Minty and Jack, the two fox terriers belonging to Alastair and Ben respectively. Minty was a temperamental little animal, as the bites on my fingers in the months to come would show. No boardroom, no PAs, no Human Resources Department. Just the smell of hops, the shouts from the men and women on the work floor down below, the clank of metal as barrels were unloaded in the yard.

Even though I already knew the business well, having looked at Meantime in one way or another for over a year now, it was still quite a jolt that Monday morning. There was a sense of the ropes slipping away from the bollards on the dock as the boat leaves the security of the port. It was a big moment in many ways. My marriage to my first wife was fragile; over the years, I'd travelled constantly around the UK and Europe as a senior beer executive, putting strains on family life, but more recently she and I had both been aware of greater tensions. With the move to Meantime, I'd bought a flat in Greenwich to work from during the week, with the plan to return to the family home in Newbury at the weekends. But in retrospect, we both knew what the likely outcome would be.

The stakes were very high for me. Six years earlier, a psychometric test carried out at SAB Miller as part of the recruitment process (suffice to say, those tests weren't a part of the Meantime culture) had forecast that, as a senior executive, I would peak by the age of 54. I had a lot to prove. I'd taken a 50 per cent pay cut to move to Meantime, in the process giving up all my rights to shares in SAB Miller plc, not an inconsiderable pot. I was gambling that the contract I'd negotiated with the board and shareholders of Meantime would reap rewards if I achieved my objective: to build the company up and sell it for at least £50m within five years. But when almost all my salary was going on supporting the family back in Newbury and servicing the hefty mortgage I'd taken out to buy the flat in Greenwich, I could feel the proximity of failure taunting me in the wings.

I've discovered over the years that the risk/reward dichotomy is a crucial element in business thinking. There is a theory about risk in business propounded by Kahneman and Tversky (1979) which goes something like this: a person's willingness to take risks is dependent on their perception of the situation. Individuals will be risk averse if they perceive themselves in a win situation, but will be risk seeking in a loss situation. Other research indicates that the propensity to take risks in business often has a correlation with the experience of the individual concerned, the number of years he or she has had to experience business life. In other words, the situation of the entrepreneur, the knowledge that he or she has built up and the personal conditions they're facing are more important factors when it comes to taking a risk than personality. What I take from that argument is that you need to be clear and honest with yourself when you are trying to evaluate your own appetite for risk.

There were all kinds of reasons why I shouldn't have taken the plunge in 2011. In doing so, I was giving up around 60,000 shares in SAB Miller plc, which would have realised about £2.5 million when that company came to be sold to ABI a few years later. I was moving out of the family home, initially just on a weekday basis, but with the clear intuition inside of me that by doing so, I was taking an irretrievable step. I'd never had a job in a small company, had spent my entire career within major public companies or global enterprises; I simply had no knowledge of what life was like on a day-to-day basis in a small, private company. If I failed to achieve what I was setting out to do, there would be massive implications for the security of the family as well as a major dent in my career, and I had no security other than my own sense of strategy that I could make this whole thing work. Failure would, to put it bluntly, be absolutely disastrous for me and for the financial stability required to provide for my family.

That's not to say I thought I *would* fail. I didn't; I've always had a positive mindset, and I've always looked for a solution when one was needed. After Dad left home when I was 13, I became even more of a tearaway, so it was no surprise when I completely flunked my A-levels: I hadn't done a stroke of work. The schoolmates I played cricket with were all readying themselves to go off to university, and Mum and my future stepdad Mike, with the best of intentions, were suggesting I get a part-time job and try re-sitting my exams a year later. I knew even then that my exam failure was entirely my fault and by the age of 18 I'd learned that life didn't reward excuses – I knew that I had to sort myself out and take ownership of my failings. I didn't fear the future and I actually felt pretty confident, given the independent lifestyle I'd developed as a teenager, that I'd turn out all right, have an enjoyable career and even make some money.

After the ignominy of opening that envelope with my A-level results in, I found myself a job for the summer at the British Gypsum plaster mine a mile away from home, working on a cleaning gang sanitising the pearlite bins on the main factory floor and deep down inside the mine cleaning industrial screws. I was used to hard work, having spent previous summers labouring on building sites for my Uncle Phil (part of my mum's family in Watford). Now I was encountering the real world which, I discovered, included unreasonable characters. One of my workmates was a Muslim lad called Akmel and he used to ask me to cover for him five times a day so he could get down on his prayer mat. I'd make extra noise clattering about with the metal plaster mixing poles while he prayed. Sadly there was a nasty shop floor bully who'd pick on Akmel whenever he could, try and hide his prayer mat, give him a slap. This guy used to have a go at me too because he didn't like the fact I defended Akmel. He'd drive a forklift over my safety helmet, trip me up on the way to the mine. Eventually, I'd had enough and I walloped the little swine with one of the mixing poles.

Bullying is one of those unlikeable human characteristics that is still all too prevalent, particularly in the workplace.

I'd had my first experience of facing up to this kind of adversity head on as a 17-year-old. The school hard nut pulled my chair out from behind me as I was sitting down in the classroom. When I got up, I went over and shoved him. He looked surprised, and interested.

'All right,' he said. 'Want to settle this tomorrow, out of school?'

I'd never really been in that situation before, so I just nodded.

'Yeah, all right then.'

The following day we met at the appointed place, a friend's garden, and surrounded by a gang of yelling kids, we beat seven bells out of each other. Maybe I ended up having the best of it, although we both broke each other's noses and both of us ended up with faces that looked like mushroom fields. The bully had a week off school. When I got home that day and pulled off my motorbike helmet, it was like ripping the strongest duct tape off your skin. Mum was appalled, tended as best she could to the wounds, gave me a royal ticking off and sent me back to school the following day. When I went in, word had obviously got around. My teacher took me aside.

'What happened to your face, Miller?' he asked me.

'Fell over at home, sir,' I said.

He and the other teachers by then had heard what had happened, but I stuck to my story. A week later, the head of sixth form, Basil Hind, told me he was making me deputy head boy and as he did so, told me it was because he liked the way I'd refused to talk about the fight. I guess he thought it was the honourable thing to do but maybe also he was grateful that I'd sorted a problem out for him?

I was making good money at the gypsum mine, probably still as much of a tearaway as I'd been while at school: some of the fitters used to take me out on their poaching trips at night, and I'd be the 'idiot' going ahead beating the bushes to stir the prey while they followed on behind with shotguns with torches strapped to them. It's incredible they didn't blow my head off. I received my first lesson in health and safety at the mine, when our foreman, who for some reason we called 'Shit Legs', caught me trying to clean the inside of a metal cylinder while the screws were still turning. He yelled at me fiercely, until I finally realised that perhaps he had a point. I'd think of him many years later when I used to wander around the bottling plant at Meantime, fearing that we might have missed a health and safety issue that could impact on someone.

Each morning as I got up and ran across the fields to reach the gates of the gypsum mine on time, I knew this wasn't going to last long; this wasn't going to be my destiny. I knew that I could make something of myself, so I walked into the local Jobcentre and asked them to find me a job that didn't involve cleaning massive metal conveyor belts with high-powered vacuums. Thankfully, they found me a place as a trainee shop manager for Barratts Shoes and, after five months of training in Derby and Chesterfield, just before my 19th birthday, I was sent north to manage a small shoe shop in Darlington.

I spent three years with Barratts. In Darlington, I lodged with one of my two staff members, Mrs Bowman, for the first four weeks. She and Miss Martin, the shop supervisor, both called me Mr Miller: the three of us never used Christian names. They were both lovely, hard-working, diligent ladies in their fifties who had worked in that shop for years and, if truth be told, they managed me as much as I managed them. While I boarded with Mrs Bowman, once out of the shop and in her home environment, the tables were turned and she became the strict housekeeper. I took a mischievous delight in leaving my underpants strewn around my room, which never failed to disappoint her. But I began to learn: stocktaking, cashing up at the end of the day, window-dressing (although I have to be honest and admit that I never mastered that art: crouched in the cramped environment of the shop front, I was more like a bull in a china shop). Painfully and slowly, I began to take on lessons about how to manage. One day when one of the ladies kept sitting down and puffing, red in the face, I joshed her, told her she was taking it a bit easy, until the other took me aside and said, 'Mr Miller, she has begun the menopause.'

That night, I had to ring my mum.

'Mum,' I asked, 'what's the menopause?'

After a year, I moved on to a bigger shop in Durham. It was 1984, smack bang in the middle of the miners' strike. The 1980s in the north of England was a tough, combative environment, battle lines drawn up by Margaret Thatcher's determination to beat the miners' union. Coming from a semi-rural upbringing in Staffordshire, it was a real shock to encounter the impact of economics and politics on every street. One day, a miner came into the shop with an old pair of shoes in a tatty box, slammed it down on the counter and demanded a refund.

'These shoes are faulty,' he said.

I turned them over.

'They're not faulty; they're old,' I replied. 'You've worn them out.'

He came up close to my face.

'Listen lad,' he said. 'Do you know what it's like trying to feed a family when you've got no money? I'm on strike. My children are starving. I want you to refund these shoes.'

I shook my head.

'I can't do it,' I told him.

He looked at me for a moment, then punched me hard in the face, knocking me to the floor. I lay there clutching my face, not fancying my chances, but yelled at him:

'Get out of my shop.' Fortunately he did.

I lived a full-on life back then. After I moved out of Mrs Bowman's lodgings, I took a room in a house owned by a bloke called Paul who had recently lost both his parents to cancer. I moved in with him together with another lodger, a nurse called Liz. I bought an old VW Beetle, would often wake up with a terrific hangover in York or Newcastle after another belting night out and have to race back to Durham to open up the shop. I was burning the candle at both ends to such an extent that I ended up with appendicitis and had to let the surgeons at Bishop Auckland hospital take the damn thing out. I remember lying on the hospital bed while a nurse prepared to shave my nether regions in preparation for surgery, and inevitably I made some cheap gag. She wasn't impressed:

'Normally with a man I'd need two razors to deal with this area, but in your case I think one is quite enough.'

At the same time – 'in the meantime' – I was learning: how to sell, how to manage, how to put in hard graft. I knew, deep down, that if I worked hard enough I would have a greater chance of maximising my limited capabilities. It wasn't particularly a money thing for me. Of course

I wanted to earn more, but more than anything I had an instinct that I could make something of myself. I was – still am, if I'm honest – very competitive; I wanted to win every game I entered. I knew that I had an innate intelligence that I hadn't tapped. I knew that I was quite commercial, and I had a strong feeling that I could encourage money to come my way. I knew that I was entrepreneurial. Above all, I knew I had the energy, the will, the desire and the determination; I wasn't going to give in. Above all I wanted to prove to myself, to my mother and to my father, that I could do it.

The thing that I didn't have back then, as a cheerful 21-year-old shoe salesman, was the time to absorb the lessons about people which, if you keep your eyes and ears open, life will teach you. Over the years since my time at Barratts, I've worked with and for some really inspiring people. They all have the same characteristics: they have energy, they are inquisitive, they have emotional intelligence, they understand the concept of humility, they are prepared to listen. Successful businesses have people with a strong set of values – I was lucky enough to have a mum who instilled those in me. She taught me to work hard, to take responsibility for myself and my actions, to deal with disappointment. If you combine all those elements together, you find that people who succeed in business always do the same thing: they put the business first and their ego last. I believe that successful business people base 85 per cent of their decisions on the needs and strategy of the business; 10 per cent of their decisions on the views of those around them; and 5 per cent of their decisions on their own desires. Unsuccessful people do the opposite (usually without knowing it) and create failure by pursuing the dictates of their own ego.

One of the crucial elements, therefore, in building your own personal business strategy is always being prepared to listen to people, to watch how other people behave and to learn from both. There are very few management techniques or theories which don't put people right up there at the top of the list, and there are very, very few successful entrepreneurs who can build genuine success without appreciating the role of the people they work with. Granted, some can succeed while riding roughshod over their colleagues, but the truth is they are few and far between and usually find themselves and the business they have created tripping up at some point because successful businesses are about the people who work within them.

As I stood in the doorway of that threadbare office in Greenwich in September 2011, I knew that I was arriving with a tapestry of experience of people and how they can combine together to achieve amazing things if the circumstances and the processes are well managed. While there was everything to play for at Meantime and we were still standing at the foot of the mountain, I had the internal equipment – the experience, the training, the attitude, the appetite for risk – to make a success of it for us all. Essentially, I knew what components we needed to build the ski lift to the top. This was my opportunity to show the world what I was really made of. Did I have something to prove? Probably. I didn't go to university at the same time as everyone else, worked my way up through the ranks of Bass and then SAB Miller, always conscious of my own relatively humble background when dealing with some of the more entitled senior members of the UK beer industry. Most people will characterise you in their minds as the person they see, not the person you are and almost never the person you could become. I suspect I had always felt throughout my career that I could achieve more than my peers suspected of me. Now, within the confines of this little brewery in south-east London, I had my chance.

I was confident too, because this was Meantime. There were countless small breweries dotted around Britain in 2011 but Meantime had some very special characteristics. In the next chapter, I'll take a look at those in more detail, to tease out specifically why this beer brand rather than any other was ready to grow. But the character of the people I was coming to work with was crucial too, starting with Alastair, the founder. Alastair Hook – or Hooky as I inevitably called him – is a complex, brilliant, creative brewer. As a South London lad, he'd discovered a passion to be a brewer and had taken himself off to Heriot-Watt University, one of the best universities to study the science of brewing, after leaving school. Then he'd moved to Germany to apprentice under some of the renowned German brewers, had learned the Continental style of brewing, which he complemented with American training too. After a variety of ventures in the British beer sector, he'd taken the plunge in 1999, with the help of some 'family and friends' money, to found Meantime on his home turf, Greenwich.

Hooky is determined, tough, resilient and highly competitive. During my four years at Meantime, most of our best decisions were taken on the golf course – where he would usually win – or the cricket pitch, which was my terrain. Whether we were skiing or rowing across the Channel for charity (which we did in 2013) or playing pool in the pub, Hooky and I never gave each other a break. Outside of sport, we rarely socialised and in fact that was one of the hallmarks of the entire team: we all bonded and worked to our very limits during the working week, but we recuperated at weekends among our own families and social circles. Hooky was a man who loved the finer things in life: excellent food, fine beer and wine, travel (he was a Germanophile after his early brewing experience there). He is passionate about making beer and, despite not having been exposed to all the skillsets required of a successful business person, he had done an incredible job in those first ten years. At one point, Meantime had been the beer of choice in the Sainsbury's *Taste the Difference* range, an achievement not to be underestimated. He'd opened two pubs in Greenwich, The Greenwich Union (known just as The Union) and The Old Brewery, to showcase Meantime beers and they were beloved of the South London craft beer aficionado. He'd created a brand and a beer which should have been doing much better than it was by 2011.

Hooky's co-founder, Ben Joseph, was different in all sorts of ways. Quick, funny, commercial, he could turn himself to many trades. At one point, he'd played bass for Desmond Dekker and his father had been a famous South London gambler. Ben was highly capable and I came to value him as the 'glue' who helped in the transformation of Meantime into the vision I held clearly in mind. He was gracious and supportive of my arrival and swiftly emerged as a powerful and reliable operations director on whom I relied more and more as we expanded our distribution rapidly. The third co-founder, Lars Huser, was a massive Dane with the hair and frame of a Viking. While he didn't operate out of the Meantime offices, he always backed me throughout my tenure.

Down on the shop floor we had similarly strong characters. Brewers like Rory, an unflappable and endlessly cheerful Zimbabwean; the Cash brothers, the tough and talented football-loving brewing experts who reported in to Hooky; Bash, the muscled Albanian who could tell where the mechanical fault on the bottling line was just by standing still and listening; talented, hard-working sales and marketing people like Alice and forceful, unique characters like brewery tour guide Big Al. We had the only man other than Hooky that I'd really listen to about beer quality, our brewer Rod Jones, who created all kinds of exotic experiments but always knew how to deliver a beer that pleased the consumer. Rod was so passionate about beer that he'd take his wife around European breweries on their summer holidays! There were immensely strong characters like Rob Hacker, who'd had a career in banking and was recruited into the Meantime sales department after he'd been spotted regularly propping up the bar in The Union, and who after my arrival turned out to be almost as strong a 'glue man' for our business as Ben Joseph. These were genuine, collaborative team workers, all passionate about the brand that Hooky had created, all committed to the South London home of Meantime and the streets which made up the square mile in which the brewery and our two pubs operated.

There was something about the place. Maybe I'd picked up on that over the previous 12 months when I'd been poking my nose into the business, but those first couple of weeks in September really brought home to me just what a great collection of people I had come to work with. Without them, of course, nothing that came to pass would have happened. Remember that great scene in *On the Waterfront* when Marlon Brando bitterly laments, 'I could've been a contender'? Well, we had what it took to be contenders, and our waterfront brewery was only going to go in one direction. The jigsaw pieces were scattered on the table; they just needed putting together.

Chapter Two

'Great Stuff, This Bass'

I have found that, in business, it's more often the questions you ask than the statements you make which determine whether you are going to succeed. The leader who walks into a room full of people and tells everyone in it what he or she thinks, then walks out again without having found out what they all think about key issues, is creating a situation of stasis. There's going to be no movement ahead, just more of the same. On the other hand, if you go into that room and start asking questions, you'll very quickly find out crucial information about how the strategy in your head can most effectively be implemented on the ground. Not just any questions: start with big, open questions, and as the answers come flying back, focus the questions down more and more, so you create a funnel effect. What comes out at the end, like a good craft beer after it's been properly matured, is the reality of what's available to you. Then you can get to work.

After three years of selling shoes in the north of

England, despite a very enjoyable social life and a string of irresponsible escapades, I knew that at the age of 21 I'd begun to understand just how much I didn't know and how I needed to expand my horizons. All my schoolmates had moved to London by now, so perhaps I needed to do the same. I'd started to ask the bigger, more open questions, but I needed to learn more and narrow down my investigations. I'd realised that I needed to learn so much: about buying, managing people, all the processes that went into making a business. With that inkling I had about my potential, I told my mum one day that I thought I needed to look beyond Barratts and maybe head down south to the 'Big Smoke' to test myself. Being the sociable person she is, she just happened to know a man called Carl Haig who was part of the Bass human resources team. Fully aware by now of my predilection for a decent pint, Mum suggested I go and see him. I put on my best suit (my only one) and presented myself for interview in Burton. Several interviews later, I was offered a job as a trainee sales manager and given my first patch in East London, and told to go out and sell the Charrington portfolio of beers, lagers, a few wines and the Britvic soft drinks range.

The Bass company in 1986 was in many ways a throwback to the grand old days of British industry. It was a massive company, listed on the FTSE 100[4] with five main divisions: brewing, pubs, hotels, Britvic soft drinks, and the leisure division, which included Coral betting shops among others. These were still the days before the government

---

4 The Financial Times Stock Exchange 100 Index (FTSE 100) is the list of the top 100 companies listed on the London Stock Exchange in terms of their market capitalisation.

stepped in three years later to create the Beer Orders[5] which broke up the brewers' monopolies, when the Big Six[6] had around 7,000 pubs each and among them controlled the English drinks industry; the idea of the free house was rare in those days. Perhaps even more so than its five main competitors, Bass was rooted in its 18th-century origins, with plush dining rooms for directors, less salubrious but still comfortable rooms for middle managers, canteens for workers. It was a throwback to a previous era in many ways and it still used that famous copyline 'Great stuff, this Bass' when I joined. It was an institution.

I settled into a shared house in Dulwich rented by my old Hanbury mate, Mike Fenwick. Mike attracted people in those days and still does. A big, cheerful fellow, he and his family – particularly his mum and dad, Eddie and Eileen – were hugely important to me as influences when I was growing up. He was still ginger haired back in those days, and had managed to achieve the singular distinction of being barred from the local kebab shop – Mike spent a year assiduously learning the patterns of the electronic quiz machines in East London and had memorised all the questions and answers; he was so successful that all the local outlets that boasted them had to keep him out. I moved into his flat together with a collection of other lads like me, some from the Midlands or the North, others from far-flung places, all come to London to 'seek their fortune'. I was the

5 The Beer Orders were a series of Statutory Instruments approved by the government in 1989 which had the effect of breaking up the ownership of the British beer industry and created a new generation of smaller pub groups and independent houses.
6 The Big Six were Whitbread, Scottish and Newcastle, Bass Charrington, Allied Breweries, Courage Imperial and Watneys.

only one who'd been working up to that point so I brought along my own television, and every time Margaret Thatcher came on, they'd hurl beer cans at the screen – these were still febrile, turbulent days and our house was filled with feisty, left-leaning youngsters. The patch I was given to work covered East Ham, West Ham, Plaistow, Walthamstow, Leyton, Isle of Dogs, Mile End Road, Bow. It was a tough area, made harder by the fact that Bass was only third or fourth in the ranking of the Big Six brewers in East London; I was put to work in an area where most of the pubs were already tied up by Bass's competitors Scottish & Newcastle and Courage. That meant that people in my East End area were used to drinking Fosters and were less familiar with our lager brand, Carling. I was selling on the back foot into free houses, working men's clubs, restaurants, bingo halls and corner shops, because this wasn't 'Bass territory'; at the same time, for the very same reason, every sale I made somehow counted for more.

For three years, I 'ripped it up'. I made it to salesman of the year twice, and won a holiday to Bali. I worked my socks off and I think some of the customers I brought in just took a shine to this eager little northern lad with his funny accent who'd always turn up on time with a smile on his face. I was beginning to learn how business worked, aided by many people but especially by a senior manager at Charrington's called Ray Loake who really set me on the path. Ray was ex-RAF, an imposing, tall man who became a bit of a father figure to me in those days. He'd get me out on the golf course at six in the morning on Saturdays, no matter what hour I'd staggered home the night before; when Ray said something, you listened. He taught me how to construct a sale, how to progress through from asking the potential customer what they needed, listening to what they said, building a solution which met their needs. When I was selling shoes, I thought my job was to persuade every person who came into the shop to buy a pair of shoes, which to an extent was reasonable because our range wasn't that broad: there were only so many shoe styles available. Now I was part of Bass Charrington, one of Britain's biggest and oldest breweries, and I had a vast range of different businesses and business owners who all had different aims and needs. At one of my early assessments, Ray told me:

'Nick, you've got to become more streetwise. You've got to understand what these people want and then find the right way to give that to them.'

Through the expert (and demanding) tutoring from Ray Loake and another significant influence on my career, Tony Baumann, as well as from my own daily experience on the ground in the East End, I learned how to sell and specifically how to manage the six key steps of selling, which are all based on listening, questioning, presentation skills with an empathy towards the customer's needs. Over time, I found that the following process formed an invaluable structure for building a sale:

1. Identify the need and the want, which are different but complement each other. Someone may have a need but not want it, or they might want something but not need it. You must identify how both sit with your potential customer, and the most effective way of doing that is by asking big, open questions. Ultimately, you should never try and sell something to

someone who doesn't really need or want it, because at the end of the day, that sale is going to come back and bite you.

2. Having identified the need, you then clarify it and develop it with the customer using your questioning and listening skills.

3. Once you've got a really good handle on why your product could benefit this potential customer, you can then offer the correct product solution.

4. Your next job is to prove that solution. Give the customer the evidence that your solution is correct: how it will impact on their cash flow, how it will bring in more customers to their bar, how it will improve their reputation. I learned some of the most important elements of presentation: tell the customer what you're going to say, then say it, then tell them what you've said.

5. Now you must overcome objections. Allow the customer to ask you questions, listen and answer truthfully. Sincerity can win sales; insincerity can lose them.

6. Finally, you must close. You can go for a direct close, which means a yes or a no, or you may discover you have a talent or penchant for one of the many different forms of closing recorded over the years: there's the 'Colombo' sale, when you lean back as though you're accepting you don't have a sale, then you come back in at the last minute with a killer line. Or the 'Half Nelson' sale, when you have them

wrapped up so tight they can only say yes. (The half nelson is a grip used in wrestling in which one fighter locks the other into a supine position with one arm holding the neck.) There are countless books written on the different forms of the close (and you should explore them all if it interests you) but as long as you use one of them effectively, then you've successfully completed the six-step sales process.

I absolutely relished this sense of opening up, of my personal horizons suddenly becoming so much wider. I was asking questions all the time, finding out more and more about how these businesses (who were my customers) wanted to grow. For example, I got to know the people who'd decided to turn an old slag heap in Becton into a ski slope. They put a case to me about how much beer they could sell the happy skiers if they had a bar at the foot of the slope and I produced a complete business case for my boss to justify Bass lending them £100,000 to build it. I worked out proposals for how we'd balance a repayment loan to them against a varying discount on the price of the beer we shipped in, and before long Becton Alps was one of my most profitable customers. It was all a long way from selling shoes in a shop in Durham.

Being streetwise wasn't just about learning the financial realities of hospitality businesses. It was also about coming to terms with the scams. The one you really had to watch out for was 'fencing': as a salesman, you meet a new customer who claims to have taken a lease on a new outlet. He places some initial small orders with you. You get to know him; he seems to trust you. You reciprocate that trust. Then after a few months, he puts in a much bigger order, and he tells you it's for a special event. You ship in a huge quantity of beer, he never pays you, you never see him again and you're left explaining to your boss why your budget is down several thousand pounds. This was one of the many specialities of the Kray twins in the 60s and 70s and no doubt I was dealing with members of their empire as I began to develop a nose for those deals it was best to walk away from.

Selling into East End outlets in London in the 1980s was, now I think back on it, a riot. I never really needed to think about stocking up on food at home because all the people I'd be visiting on my rounds would feed me out of an instinctive hospitality worker's desire to see people satisfied. Even if I didn't get a sale, a generous bingo hall owner or social club manager would insist I sit down and eat a cheese and pickle sandwich before going on my way. I grew to love the curry houses in the East End where I'd find myself sitting at Formica tables cramming my face with samosas while a generous owner looked on approvingly, having refused to buy my Carling. My overwhelming memory is of the Charrington team and customers operating like a really happy, all-encompassing and welcoming family, all of us working as part of a huge team.

I had this sense too when I went into St Thomas' Hospital on the South Bank for some tests. I'd been feeling not quite right for a while, with some pretty nasty bowel complaints, and in my usual way I'd ignored it, preferring to plough ahead with the job in hand. But one or two of the friendly and supportive people I worked with at this time pressured me into going for a check-up. The faces on the medical team once they'd checked me over were pretty serious: there was a 10 per cent chance I had cancer, and a 90 per cent chance I was suffering from Crohn's disease. Well, the good news was it wasn't the former, but the not-so-good news was that it was definitely Crohn's, which affects me to this day. It's a rare illness: only 0.17 per cent of the UK population suffer from it. It's a lifelong illness and if you're unlucky enough to get it, the symptoms usually arrive in early adulthood: diarrhoea, stomach cramps, tiredness, weight loss. There's no real way of dealing with it other than trying to work out which foods tend to bring on an inflammation, which sadly were all the things I liked, including the delicious curries my customers would serve me in the East End.

I spent four weeks in hospital and was visited by colleagues and customers alike, reflecting that family sense of work at the time. I was endlessly inventive in ways of combating the boredom of being stuck in hospital: at one point, I discovered that the doctors' restaurant served much better food than we were getting on the ward, and one day I 'borrowed' a white coat and stethoscope and snuck in for a decent meal. I also crept out with another fellow on my ward, a Brixton flower seller, for a sneak pint at a pub round the corner, and was told off in no uncertain terms by the ward sister. I had another few weeks of recovery time after the operation and then I was back on the job and was gratified that I hadn't lost a single account. Every one of my customers on my patch was incredibly supportive, asking how I was, giving me a pat on the back.

Over the years since, I've made a conscious point about not letting the disease hold me back. The uncomfortable physical symptoms just became something that I deal with; once I'd understood the terms of the disease, it seemed obvious to me that there was no point in making a fuss about it – how would that help me? How would that help me build my career? Over the years, hardly anyone has known I suffer from it. Even today, as my wife Em will attest with a bit of eye-rolling, I'll happily hoover up a full Indian meal with some beers, fully aware of the inevitable consequences. I've tried to manage my illness through a positive mindset. It's what my mum would have said: you get on with it. You can let it beat you, or you beat it.

The disease didn't get in the way of my work in London's East End. I remember the time when I was standing behind the bar of a working men's club which I'd successfully converted into a Bass Charrington customer. I had two chaps in to fit our nice new shiny taps on the bar and in walked the salesman from Scottish & Newcastle who I'd edged out. He walked straight up to the bar, clocked how I was replacing his taps with mine, and said:

'You little toerag. Think you can steal my customer? I'll teach you a lesson.'

He was about to swing a punch when the two fitters, Henry and Keith, stood up from where they were working behind me, looked at him and said:

'Sorry mate, what was that you said you were going to do?'

The S&N salesman slunk off and we all laughed (me with relief). The family had my back.

It felt like a world where you could just crack on and make your own luck because everyone was really part of a big family who looked out for each other. It was hard work and you were told in black and white when your performance was lacking, but you always felt like someone would look out for you. It was a world filled with memorable characters, particularly the draymen, the heavily unionised transport workers who shifted beer around the city. One of their favourite games was to stop off on the Embankment, lower one of the long, slim carbon dioxide bottles (to which they had added rudimentary fins) into the water, open up the tap and see if they could hit a boat the other side of the Thames as the escaping gas powered it incredibly dangerously across the water.

I also remember the draymen 'kidnapping' me one Friday evening. I'd finished work and was looking forward to heading off home to go out for the night. One of the draymen called me over as I walked across the yard towards my car.

'Nick, come over here; Charlie wants a word with you.'

He was standing by the coach and was pointing at the door.

'He's in there, just go and have a word with him, he wants to mention something to you.'

Charlie was the boss of the draymen's gang.

'Can't it wait till Monday?' I called back, getting out my car keys.

'Only a minute, Nick, just go and have a word.'

So I climbed up into the coach and immediately the door was slammed behind me and the engine started.

'Oy!' I yelled, but I was drowned out by the laughter. It turned out the Charrington's draymen were due to play darts against the Alton Brewery in Hampshire and they were a man short. Several hours later, having won the match but now considerably worse for wear, I was dropped back in Silvertown.

The other element I learned from those splendid draymen was how much you can learn from the people you work with. They were always on the ground, moving around London, seeing and experiencing things with a particular eye to the beer market, and many was the time one of them would give me a useful bit of information about a potential new customer or a potential problem with an existing customer. Your progress in business benefits from listening to those in your team, no matter how high or low their position in the corporate structure.

That was one thing I smelled in that ramshackle Meantime office on Blackwall Lane: it wasn't streetwise. The people who made it up were in their own different ways very streetwise – plenty of South London geezers and gals, as I used to say. But the business itself wasn't streetwise. My new colleagues were brilliant in their own way: Hooky as a creative and passionate brewer, Ben as an accomplished Jack-of-all-trades, the salesmen I inherited like Rob Hacker and Conor Tait, all delivering as well as they knew how to the reasonably slim customer list. But the team as a whole was lacking the commercial imperative which I've come to believe you only develop over time. It is possible to create and sell a consumer brand without 'learning the ropes' over the years like I did, but those cases are few and far between; most successful consumer brands are built on the back of years of experience of trade and consumer marketing. If you don't have that level of experience, it can often pay over the long term to bring it into the business through effective recruitment.

Over the four years I spent at Meantime, it was this awareness which kept me in a relatively lonely position as the boss. Don't get me wrong: we rapidly became a tight family and to this day I keep in close touch with most of my ex-colleagues, talk regularly on the phone about what we're up to now, meet up when we can to share a beer. We were passionately committed to the brand; we devoted all our waking hours to it. But my colleagues also loved it in a very emotional and sometimes uncommercial way; they'd grown Meantime within the beautiful Royal Borough of Greenwich and the brand was genuinely a core element of their lives. The Meantime people were deeply engaged in that part of south-east London, and they all knew people who loved to sup a pint at The Union. I came to share those feelings but I never allowed them to overcome the real reason I'd taken the plunge and joined.

One of the many learning experiences I'd had in the years in the corporate world leading up to the Meantime period was discovering how to behave as I'd climbed the ladder from one job to the next. There you are, with a fancy new job title, and you're thinking to yourself: 'Well, I still feel like the same bloke. I know who I am. What's the expectation of me?' And what I learned was that the shadow you cast gets much, much longer the more you get promoted. As the boss, absolutely everything you say and do will be analysed to death by more and more people inside the organisation. The ability to be taken at face value diminishes the more senior you get. So I learned that I had to change my behaviour: the way I behaved as a rough and ready salesman in the early days of my career at Bass, diving naked into swimming pools or always being the last person to bed at a conference… those days were long gone. (Although, if I'm honest, they could resurface every now and then...) They were definitely behind me after attending a course on presenting during my later years at Bass which was run by an actor from RADA, the Royal Academy of Dramatic Arts. In my usual manner, I'd gone into the course assuming I could 'wing it', having made more presentations in my career than I liked to recall. But this smart chap took me aside and said:

'Nick, you've got a problem.'

'What's that?'

'You don't know how to pretend to be a Good King. You're always the court jester.'

He went on to give me an insight into how actors performed at the Globe Theatre in London. At each of the four corners of the theatre were signs showing North, East, South, West. One represented air, telling actors they should always breathe. One stood for earth, meaning they should ground themselves and hold their stance strongly. The third was fire, inspiring the actors to be filled with passion. The final one, water, reminded them always to be in flow.

'You need to remember that, Nick,' he concluded. 'Your audience, the people who work for you, need to believe in you as the Good King. You need to ground yourself and not jump around like a March hare. They've got enough jokers at home.'

It was a lesson I took very much to heart and I thought of him often once I'd landed in Greenwich, almost a stone's throw from Shakespeare's Globe on the South Bank. I had a role to play here, among these really impressive and committed people at Meantime, and I never allowed myself to forget it.

A year before, as the managing director of Miller Brands

UK (the name obviously a coincidence), I was in a strong position. Miller Brands UK was a relatively recent corporate structure, effectively the UK distribution company for the hugely powerful SAB Miller global brewing group. I'd joined it in 2005 after 19 years at Bass, tasked by the new UK managing director, Gary Whitlie, to help him as sales director build distribution in the UK for SAB's products, including Bass/Coors, Peroni, Pilsner Urquell, Miller Genuine Draft, Kozel and Tyskie.[7] SAB, originally formed in the late 19th century as the South African Brewery, had become a huge global player under CEO Graham Mackay, with its strength mainly located in Africa, Eastern Europe and the Far East. Now, in 2005, they had decided to enter the UK market and I joined it under Gary when there were just eight employees. By the time I left, six years later, we had 180 employees and as a team had created a multi-million-pound business on the back of the development of Peroni.

We transformed Peroni Nastro Azzurro from its position as a relatively niche and food-biased Italian lager into the country's most profitable premium lager and, in many ways, it was my training ground for the Meantime experience. But as MD of Miller Brands UK, my job also was to cover the entire range of SAB's consumer offering and I'd identified a potential strategic weakness in our portfolio. What if Peroni's dramatic rise were to plateau; what if it reached some kind of market saturation? How would I continue to grow the group business? The answer was obvious: we would need another consumer offering with the potential to grow as strongly as Peroni. I had a lot of firepower at

7 Kozel and Tyskie were both Polish lagers, popular with the Polish workers who had begun to be more of a visible presence in the UK.

my disposal in 2010: SAB Miller was one of the biggest drinks groups in the world and I was in good favour on the back of the Peroni performance. So I was able to invest money in working with top consultants to analyse carefully the potential within the UK drinks landscape. Where was the next Peroni?

The answer, first, had to be a premium ale. The last thing Miller Brands needed to do was to compete against itself with another lager, and Peroni still had a long way to run. So where could the opportunity lie within British beer? We set down some key criteria:

- The beer had to be capable of performing as a 'premium' brand.[8] The amount of marketing spend required to boost a standard ale within such a competitive market would be prohibitive, even for a successful group like SAB Miller.

- This meant that we needed to analyse the entire British brewing sector against what is called a WAMP measure: weighted average market pricing, all based on beer industry statistics. We needed to identify brands which could justify a premium price.

- What were the components of a brand which could deliver in this way? It was a complex mix of brand character, production capability, cost of goods, potential marketing reach and ability to grow.

Having established these criteria, I spent a couple of

---

8 The beer industry segregated genres of beer into alcohol by volume (ABV). Anything below 4.5 per cent ABV was 'standard'; anything above was 'premium'. I always preferred to distinguish them on price.

months with a really bright team of consultants analysing every brewery in the country. We looked at well-known brands as well as obscure ones. It didn't matter at that stage: all were forced down through the same consultancy set of equations. And after two months of hard and fascinating work, we identified a beer brand which had all the characteristics we required to become an explosive performer if it were brought into the SAB Miller stable. That brand was Meantime. This was without me ever meeting Hooky, without me swapping jokes with Ben in the warehouse, without me even visiting The Union to order a pint. The numbers told the story, but only part of the story. The rest came from an understanding of the beer consumer.

Compared to my 'Wild West' days of selling Carling Black Label into bingo halls in Leytonstone in the 1980s, beer consumption by 2010 had changed dramatically. In the 1980s, most people still went to either pubs or social clubs to drink beer. They smoked in them too, spent a bit of time putting cash into fruit machines, but mostly went to and from the bar holding pints of beer. In today's very different world, they're known as 'wet pubs', but in the 1980s, they were just pubs. On the whole, people didn't drink beer at home unless it was an occasion like the FA Cup final or a birthday. They went to the pub or the club and they ordered beer at the bar.

By 2010, the landscape was very different. There was no smoking in pubs for a start. The deregulation the government had brought in in 1990 with the Beer Orders meant that the Big Six's grip on the nation's pubs had collapsed; now there was a wide range of pub and bar groups and more free houses, and more and more of these were widening their consumer offering with food, posh soft drinks like flavoured sparkling water and an ever-growing wine and cocktail list. Consumers were encouraged to feel more and more empowered about the drinks they ordered at the bar, and they increasingly liked to broadcast their own sense of identity through the drinks they consumed. They were using this new tool called the Internet to find out what was available elsewhere, to expand the range of their tastes and increasingly to compare prices. They were travelling wider and further than their parents had, and this too informed their tastes. And the pub and bar environment was now becoming much more female friendly, with chains like All Bar One establishing light, open spaces where women could feel more relaxed, a world away from the traditional male, sticky-carpeted, dark and smelly public bar.

Pubs and bars also had to compete now against the home environment. When I started out in the business, almost 90 per cent of all beer was bought in a pub or club; now, less than half of it was bought that way and most beer was bought from a shop to take home or to the park. Supermarkets had entered the fray, and throughout the summer months would be running promotions to tempt consumers into the garden or the park to barbecue a few pieces of chicken into inedible black shapes accompanied by a box of beers. You didn't have to go to the pub now to meet people – you could share a beer with friends and family anywhere you liked. The pub had to work harder to draw people in and one of the key ways it could do that was to flatter and satisfy the desires of its particular demographic target consumer.

This was where Meantime scored so highly on our complex analysis of the market back in 2010. The numbers we crunched demonstrated that all the key brand and financial metrics were in place: production, cost of goods, capacity, imagery, potential to price at a premium level. It didn't matter that it wasn't currently delivering on all those metrics; it had the potential to deliver. But just as importantly, if not more so, the brand had the capability of satisfying a consumer desire to 'trade up' in terms of ordering a pint at the bar. In this new competitive world of pubs and bars with multiple ownerships, in which consumers would be looking to have more of an individual experience as a drinker rather than just sinking eight pints of pale, there were distinct characteristics of the kind of beer which might hit the spot.

The old real ale/CAMRA[9] type of beer wasn't going to work in this respect. All our research demonstrated clearly that the devotion to old-world cask beers produced by likeable men with beards and ill-fitting clothing was highly unappealing to women, families and younger metropolitan professionals. It smacked of all the wrong things: anti-fashion, elitist, mysterious, heavy, sombre and, above all, it was served warm. What our new generation of beer consumers wanted was something contemporary, fresh, strong, vibrant and communicable. The Americans had been developing this for some time now. They called it craft beer. And they served it fresh and cold.

Our research showed that consumers perceived craft beer as different to real ale; they appeared to sense that craft beer was as different to real ale as the Leon healthy fast food

---

9 The Campaign for Real Ale was formed in 1971 as a voluntary consumer organisation to promote the virtues of 'real' or traditional ale as opposed to keg beers and lagers.

takeaway brand was to KFC or McDonald's. Craft beer was made by artisans; real ale was brewed by old men. Craft beer was about playfulness and experimentation; real ale was about solidity and consistency. Craft beer liked to tell exciting new stories; real ale was perceived to be drunk by old men. I know these generalisations will annoy some people but I'm talking from a consumer marketing perspective, talking about the way real people feel. (If it makes you feel any better, my favourite beer of all time is Timothy Taylor's Landlord, and you don't get much more traditional than that! I love cask ale and was weaned on it in Burton.) Yet however keenly we examined and explored the competitive landscape, the one thing we and almost every other beer company avoided doing was knocking the opposition. It's a truism of product marketing that consumers don't like to be told of shortcomings in one brand by another; they prefer to be encouraged to buy your product through other means. As I say, with one or two exceptions, nobody in my industry ever denigrated a rival product in public.

By 2010 the American craft beer sector was thriving, particularly in metropolitan areas on the east and west coasts. The young and thrusting executives now gathering in San Francisco to service the companies of Silicon Valley associated craft beer with modernised concepts of the American heartland. It was a freedom brand and this idea of freedom appealed to a new British generation. Youngsters here didn't want to drink their dad's beer, for a start. Ever-youthful 40-year-olds would want to mimic the social behaviour of 30-year-olds just to keep that idea of youth alive in their heads. When I was starting out, 40-year-olds reckoned they'd turned a corner in life; by 2011, that age group reckoned they were still 'happening'. Another example of how crucial it is to understand your customer and identify the market opportunity.

All our research back then indicated that we could achieve a success similar to the American model with a British craft beer, a beer that combined flavour and strength with a comprehensible and attractive story relevant to young men and women in their twenties, thirties and forties. These young people wanted to broadcast a message about themselves with the clothes they wore, the food they ate and the beer they drank. We needed a beer that was primarily aimed at the on-trade with a combination of keg and bottle offerings;[10] Miller Brands UK was a business which had worked incredibly well with pubs, bars and clubs with Peroni, and we weren't about to change that by suddenly focusing all our attention on supermarkets and the off-trade, important though they were. We needed a beer which could tell a story at the bar, which could subsequently translate in time to increased off-trade growth as consumers elected to take their new favourite beer home.

Other elements were factored into our calculations at this time. We knew that consumers not only wanted an authentic and distinctive story at the bar which would reflect their own view of themselves; they also wanted to be seen to be supporting local products, cutting down on environmentally unfriendly miles, boosting indigenous artisans.

---

10 The beer industry uses a number of terms for the containers its product is stored in. The keg is a pressurised metal barrel with a valve at one end, used to store and dispense beer which has some element of carbonation. The cask is a wooden or metal barrel used to store ale which is not carbonated. Cans and bottles are used to transport both carbonated beer and real ales.

Our research indicated that the support for a premium beer would be strongest in London and the South-East – the further north you went in Britain, the more likely the consumer was to stick to his or her traditional ale of choice. So our London and South-East consumers would in Meantime have the perfect geographical location to focus their thoughts upon: Greenwich, the home of Greenwich Mean Time, the home of Meantime. See how smart Hooky had been ten years before when he came up with the name?

We also knew that our target consumers were prepared to experiment in interesting ways, keen to pair a quality beer with food in ways which previous generations would never have considered. In the old days, matching stout with oysters was about the only time you'd get a beer drinker to talk about food matching; now, you could genuinely have a conversation with a consumer about how sometimes a wheat beer can cut into the acidity of a fish dish better than a Sauvignon Blanc. This willingness to experiment could be eased into new flavours, and in the same way as the Belgians have traditionally been happy to explore all kinds of flavours in their beers, we discovered that this new generation of consumers could be stimulated by the same sense of adventure. Raspberry beer, anyone? (Meantime's raspberry ale brewed by Hooky turned out to be a firm consumer favourite.)

Finally, we needed to be sure that our key on-trade partners would be willing to come along for the ride. We'd convinced them with Peroni as a premium lager, and everyone had made plenty of money from that. If Miller Brands UK decided to venture into premium beer, would our on-trade partners trust us that we could bring the consumer along in the same way? The Young's chain of pubs was the perfect example: probably the key customer for Miller Brands UK alongside others like Pizza Express and Mitchells & Butlers.[11] We would need to be sure that we could have a positive conversation with Young's about the idea of installing a premium ale in their pubs which had a higher price point than they were used to. This relationship with retail customers is something which I'll spend more time on later in the book, as it is such a vital element of product marketing to consumers. In particular, we'll look at the distinction between push and pull marketing, how as a brand owner you are helping your retail customer (such as Young's) to push your brand at their consumers in the pubs, and how you're giving those retail customers confidence by the pull marketing you are doing, creating interest among consumers by brand awareness marketing.

I'd summarise this entire research exercise we conducted for Miller Brands in 2010 by referencing Harvard Business School professor Michael Porter (2004), who outlined what he called the Five Forces that make up the competitive environment and influence the likely profitability of any consumer sector. It's well worth seeking out his book to examine how he defined those five forces: Competitive Rivalry, Supplier Power, Buyer Power, Threat of Substitution, Threat of New Entry.

What we were doing in 2010, therefore, was using strategic thinking such as this to explore the commercial

---

11 Mitchells & Butlers is a restaurant, pub and bar group established in the UK in 1898 and today one of the country's largest operators of such outlets with over 1,700 to its name. Their outlet brands include O'Neills, Harvester, Toby Carvery and All Bar One.

landscape for Miller Brands and to evaluate whether there was an opportunity for a second premium offering to follow on from Peroni. Another way of using strategic thinking to evaluate your competitive opportunity is summarised really well by Cliff Bowman and David Faulkner in their book *Competitive and Corporate Strategy* (1996). They came up with the insight that competitive advantage is more powerful than a cost advantage, because the strategic positioning which the former gives you provides a much stronger foundation for positioning your product in the market. Famously, they encapsulated this insight in their book as the Bowman Strategy Clock, thus:

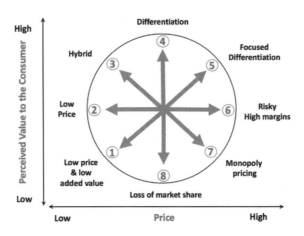

The Bowman Strategy Clock (Bowman and Faulkner 1996)

As you go around the clock, you can see how their insight makes such sense. At position one, where you have a low price and a low consumer perception of value, you're in a particularly weak competitive position, with price reductions virtually your only option. At two, value to the consumer is greater but your price is still low, so you are likely to see mass market products here, sold at a low price and offering the brand owner low profits per unit. By the time you get around to point five on the clock, you're in the sector where luxury and exclusive brands reside, offering a high-quality product at a high price, very much the kind of point on the clock where Peroni had sat. But as you continue your way around the clock, the consumer values your product less and less, making your high price point more and more risky.

All these considerations of strategy were ploughed into the research project which I undertook at Miller Brands UK during the summer of 2010. I was excited about the conclusion we'd reached, convinced by the hard numbers and the extensive consumer research that Meantime could be brought into the SAB Miller family and grown with the same explosive results as we'd achieved with Peroni lager. I hadn't ventured at this stage to open up any discussions with the board and shareholders of the brewery because I needed first to get a green light from the European head of operations for SAB Miller – in other words, my boss, the guy who reported to Graham Mackay, the remarkable South African entrepreneur who had led South African Breweries to become the global force it was when I joined in 2005.

My boss in 2010 was a Canadian Uruguayan who ran the Western Europe Trading Entities for SAB Miller. He was effective for the group in all kinds of ways, but oddly for me, because I've always had a great relationship with my bosses and learned from them all too, he and I never got on. There may have been an element of him thinking that I'd got too big for my boots with the success of Peroni, but having marshalled together what I believed was a slam-dunk, watertight case for why SAB Miller should attempt to acquire Meantime, he refused me point blank. Case closed.

What happened next is an important theme of this book: the influence of luck upon a well-developed strategy. All the work I'd put into preparing that proposal looked like it had been in vain; my boss had chucked it in the bin in that ruthless manner which some 'pigeon bosses' will always adopt: they fly in out of the blue, shit all over you and fly off again. I knew the conclusions my team and I had come to were correct because by then I'd had 25 years in the industry and I'd assembled the case with some of the smartest consultants in the country, but I wasn't in a position to be able to do anything about it. My job was running Miller Brands UK, keeping it on course, delivering profits. I was very much told: stick to your knitting. Whether you call it luck or chance or something to do with the way you live your life, it turned out that my love of cricket provided me with a solution. In the shape of 'Creepy'.

Stephen Crawley is someone who's played a very important role in my career. He is not in any sense a creepy man – he's sociable, an excellent networker, a fixer of corporate matters, not a bad cricketer and a man with some highly unusual and entertaining party tricks – but in my world, if your surname is Crawley, you're going to be nicknamed Creepy. I didn't give him the name; the whole industry calls him Creepy and he'd be offended if I didn't use it in this book. So how did Creepy play a part at this crucial point in my career? I'd first met him several years before on the cricket field, playing for one hospitality industry team against the other, and over the years we bumped into each other on different cricket fields, but never in a corporate setting. But now, after the setback of my European boss smacking me on the back of the head and telling me to walk away from the acquisition proposal I'd prepared, Creepy played a blinder. It turned out that he was a non-executive director of Meantime Brewery.

Over the late summer and early autumn of 2010, I spoke off the record to Creepy as we met outside of one cricket pavilion or another about my frustration at not being able to pursue the Meantime opportunity with SAB Miller. He, in return, began to confide in me about some of the challenges the board and shareholders were facing at the brewery. Hooky had formed the business ten years before with friends and family money, but in 2009 they'd decided to expand and bring in outside investment. They'd raised £3.4 million under the terms of the government's Enterprise Investment Scheme (EIS), which allowed investors to claim back substantial amounts of the investment they made in tax breaks.

The EIS has been a successful route for many companies over the years to raise cash from private individuals. If you're someone who's had a reasonably successful career and you have built up enough personal wealth to be having to pay the Inland Revenue some tax every year, it's quite gratifying to be able to reduce that bill while at the same time speculating on a growing business. There's only one condition: the terms of the scheme can encourage investors to seek an exit after three years because that's the period they are obliged by HMRC to hold their investment for in order to qualify for the tax relief. The government's idea is that this encourages investment money to stay in the business for a long enough time to allow it to have a positive effect. The only trouble with this is that many such investors, enjoying the fun and thrills of early-stage investing, will feel the itch to make a new investment in a new company and will want to pull their money out of the first company once the three-year point is passed. So companies which attract EIS investment in some ways are putting themselves on an inevitable path towards either selling the business or buying out the shareholders because those shareholders won't want to stay in indefinitely.

Creepy began to tell me that the investors who'd come in the previous year were concerned that Meantime wasn't on a path either to achieve a sale or for the board to have sufficient cash to buy them out. The financial year for 2010 had shown a loss before tax of £600,000; there wasn't a clear on-trade strategy to expand into pubs and the off-trade sales of bottles had plateaued; Hooky, who had achieved some outstanding things over the previous ten years, was by his own admission tired and uncertain about strategic direction. Most importantly, the £3.4 million had all been spent on building a new brewery, moving from its original location in an industrial unit opposite Charlton Athletic's football ground to its new and current home in Blackwall Lane in Greenwich and by investing in some top-of-the-range brewing kit.

I was arguing against Creepy, telling him that the current sense of treading water wasn't the important thing; what I'd discovered through my research was the incredible potential of the brand. Under the right hands, it could really leap forwards. But Creepy was worried. As a non-executive member of the board, an advisor effectively to both the directors and the senior shareholders, he was responsible for helping to find solutions. What he told me was that the bigger shareholders who had come in in 2009 were beginning to express disquiet; they wanted to see progress.

'But you don't get it,' I kept saying to him, my attention for once pulled away from the action on the crease. 'It's got everything. It's a fantastic brand; it just needs someone to grab it by the neck and run it properly.'

Creepy had had enough. Either that, or it was his turn to bat. I remember him standing up and looking down at me:

'Well if you're so bloody clever,' he said, 'why don't you come and run it?'

Chapter Three

One for the Team

Cricket, in my humble opinion, is the finest sport in the world. When I was a schoolboy, I did sometimes fool myself into thinking I could make it as a professional. I was a good cricketer, and I got as far as playing for the county in the under-19s, but deep down even then I knew I didn't really have what it took to become a proper professional sportsman. That crucial combination of physical strength, stamina and skill combined with the mental discipline you need to reach the top in sport; I knew even as a teenager I didn't have all of them. But what I love about the game is how it's taught me over the years about core values which apply as much to life as they do to business. More than any other sport, in my view, cricket celebrates the team while at the same time allowing the individual to flourish. In football, of course, the team is important as a whole – the defender is no less significant than the striker – but cricket somehow emphasises the team more while at the same time allowing the bowler who takes five wickets for just ten runs to have his moment of glory. Other sports veer towards highlighting individual roles; cricket is the ultimate team sport while still providing a stage for individual excellence. It's a sport which attracts people from all walks of life.

Despite my fairly thorough criticisms about the way it was operating, I picked up early on that Meantime was a team business and Hooky should take plenty of credit for instilling that philosophy before I ever came on the scene. There was no sense of hierarchy; there was no feeling among staff, whatever their role, that they could not voice an opinion on operations. If the Cash Brothers – the two tough-looking Chelsea supporters who both worked on the shop floor among the mashing tuns and the fermentation tanks – felt that Hooky wasn't making a correct decision, they'd tell him. And these were often complex discussions. Hooky was never going to be satisfied with the traditional British method of mashing[12] at a stable temperature; he imported all his knowledge from his training in Germany so that every beer Meantime produced was the result of a sophisticated stepped mashing process in steam-jacketed mash tuns with careful monitoring of varying temperatures. Subtle, delicate, sophisticated: this was a hallmark of Meantime but it was also a testament to the remarkable team spirit which bound everyone together. Everyone insisted on quality.

Sport will also teach you that a team can have all those qualities in spades and yet still lose matches. My job, in September 2011, was to get us in shape to win the league.

It took a year from the period of consultancy research

---

12 The brewing process in which the milled malt is mixed with hot water. This is normally done in a big container called a mash tun, with about three parts of water to one part of malt. (See Appendix.)

I'd initially carried out at Miller Brands, when I'd identified Meantime as a brand of significant interest, for me to come on board. I spent the first few months chatting with Creepy at cricket matches, and it was only when he finally came out with the throw-down-the-gauntlet challenge that I really began to consider walking away from a career with SAB Miller.

My mentor at Miller Brands was a highly talented man called Gary Whitlie, a finance director who had been tasked by Graham Mackay to build the SAB Miller brand in the UK and who had in turn hired me in 2005, initially as a sales director. Gary had been my advisor and counsellor as I progressed rapidly at SAB, moving from sales director to sales and marketing director and ultimately taking over from Gary in 2008 as managing director on the back of the Peroni performance. Gary's advice and intelligent instruction helped me enormously as I learned to deal with the corporate realities of having a pan-European boss who would habitually fly in without notice and dump on me. Gary was, and still is, a powerful presence: he was born a Geordie, but his family had emigrated to what was then called Rhodesia and he'd fought in the Rhodesian Army. After a spell in the merchant navy, he'd funded his way through accountancy exams and joined SAB, working his way up through the ranks until he became one of the most senior figures in the whole organisation. Never a man to shout, Gary could just raise an eyebrow and you'd know you'd been put in your place. I learned many crucial lessons under Gary, one of the most important being to remember the fluctuations in currency when operating internationally. Businesses which work across more than one country have to be prepared to deal with the consequences of currency changes which, unless prepared for by the process of 'hedging',[13] can mean that overnight your raw materials are costing you a lot more than you planned. We were hit once by a currency fluctuation at Miller Brands against which we hadn't covered ourselves, and were lucky to emerge unscathed.

I vividly remember how I heard about my promotion to be MD of Miller Brands UK. Gary and I were always close, and knew each other's families and enough about each other's character to consider ourselves friends, which we remain to this day. Miller Brands was a slick machine by 2008 – smart offices, professional PA backup, attractive bars on all floors to allow us to relax with an SAB product or to entertain a client. But for a few days, I sensed that Gary was avoiding me. Normally, we'd be in and out of each other's offices, or sitting down at one of the office bars at the end of the day to talk about work issues. All week he'd somehow kept out of my line of sight. I remember feeling that the week had gone well – as sales and marketing director I'd been all over the country pushing hard at our targets on Peroni – and I poked my head round the door of his office after lunch one Friday.

'Gary, I fancy a POETS today.' (You know what the acronym stands for? Piss Off Early, Tomorrow's Saturday.) I planned to get back to Newbury early and set up some activities with the kids for the weekend.

He looked up, the first time he'd looked at me all week.

'No you're not,' he said. 'I want you in here for your one-to-one at four o'clock.'

---

13 A foreign exchange hedge transfers the foreign exchange risk from the trading company to a business that carries the risk, such as a bank.

Bugger, I thought. Oh well.

So at four o'clock I went in to see him.

'I don't want to talk about what you've been doing this week,' he said straight away. 'I'm sorry I've been avoiding you. I've had to take some decisions. SAB wanted you to go to Hungary to take over country management there but I've overruled them and told them I'll go, and you can take over from me here as managing director. You're in charge of SAB Miller for the whole of the UK now. Congratulations.'

He went on to explain his decision. He liked Hungary, his second wife Elaine was a South African he'd met while previously working in Hungary, and he was nearing the end of his career so he didn't mind uprooting for a while. But he knew that my first wife, the mother of my kids, would have refused to up sticks and move to Europe and so, in a very real sense, he was protecting me by taking the job in my place.

'You'll have to go and look after another country at some point,' he finished, 'but for now you can stay here, finish the work on Peroni and raise your kids.'

Those who perhaps haven't experienced that much corporate life can sometimes be dismissive of it, assuming that it's all grey, faceless people working in big buildings. But when something like that happens, you're genuinely humbled by the humanity of an individual like Gary Whitlie, who had clearly wrestled with his conscience all week trying to work out what was best for him, what was best for me, what was best for the company. And because he's both a smart and very decent human being, he managed to achieve all three.

What he meant was, in a massive global corporation

like SAB Miller, senior executives were expected to move globally every few years to get a better insight into the international operations of the group. Someone like me, a guy in his early forties, would be expected to do at least one major international 'gig' in his career. So when, two years later, my European boss squashed all my plans for SAB to acquire Meantime, and Creepy taunted me with the prospect of leaving to run the company instead, I had a pretty clear idea of the balance of options.

If I stayed at SAB, I'd have to spend a period of my career abroad at some point and that wouldn't sit well with my family. And at the same time, my appetite for risk, which has always been a strong component for me, would be stifled. Alternatively, I could build my future in this country; I could plunge myself into a situation of absolute risk by leaving SAB and going to join this pugnacious little brewery by the Thames.

I would move to Greenwich with an armoury of management and business strategy which I'd collected from direct experience over the years. By this point in my career, I'd been working for 25 years, had some truly inspirational bosses and had studied business theory alongside my work. I was going to a small business with the clear objective of turning it around, and the man who for me best summarised the strategic process of change was John Kotter (2012), another Harvard Business School professor. He set out eight steps in the process of change and they are steps which can be used just as much in analysing your own career and situation as they can be useful in considering the development of an organisation. Briefly, the eight steps are:

1. **Increase urgency**. Identify potential threats, and then create discussion among participants on the likely impact of those threats, and include your shareholders and other stakeholders in those conversations. If there are urgent issues facing your business, the entire team needs to be encouraged to take them seriously.

2. **Build a guiding team**. Identify who are the people best placed around you to initiate and guide through change and build a team around them. Going back to the previous personnel model about energy and skills, there are always going to be a few really inspirational people who you can trust to empower and motivate their colleagues.

3. **Develop the vision**. Define core values, recognise the ultimate vision, ensure that teams responsible for implementing change can describe this vision accurately. Values and vision, while they sound a bit like corporate-speak, are in fact the core elements of a business's health and you really want your team to have them uppermost in their minds all the time.

4. **Communicate vision**. Create a comprehensible means of communicating this vision and enable others to challenge it constructively. You never want to be the leader who walks into a room, makes an announcement and then walks out again. Effecting change is a collaborative process, which is a slightly pompous way of saying a much simpler thing: keep close to your colleagues and work with them openly.

5. **Empower action.** Continually check for the existence of barriers or people who are resistant to change. Reward those who support it and always try to give people SMART objectives: Specific, Measurable, Achievable, Realistic, Timely. One of the things I learned when I came to manage salespeople was the need to 'remove rocks': if there is something or someone stopping your salesperson from selling, then remove that block.

6. **Create short-term wins.** By creating wins early on, you build a sense of mission and achievability. By giving a series of shorter-term goals, you make the longer-term goal more achievable. There's a saying for this: How do you eat an elephant? In bite-size chunks.

7. **Consolidate.** Always analyse achievements along the way and reward success. It's easy inside an organisation to take achievements for granted, but since most business achievements result from team effort, then it's a great chance to celebrate the team.

8. **Make change permanent.** Ensure everyone is able to discuss changes that have been achieved and ensure that all the organisation's leaders endorse them. We incorporated this step at Meantime with regular 'town halls', where everyone was allowed to discuss strategy and progress.

It's worth exploring the extent to which you can apply this useful model to the conditions of your own life and career as well as the organisation in which you're working. Both, I've found, benefit from such strategic analysis. Overall, I've found that your ability to progress in life and in your career owes less to your own originality and uniqueness and more to your ability to learn from experience and from the advice of others. That's why I think that making use of models like Kotter is so important when it comes to planning business: by understanding how others have performed well before, you can rely on such evidenced systems to make a success of your own activities.

Kotter's Eight Steps were certainly well to the forefront of my mind when I finally came to take the reins at Meantime in 2011. The company had a strong board of powerful characters and we'd need to embrace a new future together as a team if we were going to win. The board consisted of Hooky, Creepy, Ian Colletts (a chartered accountant who acted as the company's finance director and also looked after the interests of the company's biggest shareholder, Bill Bottriell, who had invested during the 2009 fundraising) and Tony Carson (another investor from the 2009 round, a hugely successful and charismatic retail entrepreneur). Initially, I talked to Creepy, Bill, Ian and Tony because Hooky was taking a few months out of the business to recharge his batteries. The others all told me how much they loved the brand but how concerned they were that things weren't going in the right direction.

Every one of those board members and senior shareholders played a winning role for me and for the company over the next four years. Bill Bottriell, who acted as an observer on the board given his status as the most prominent shareholder, is a remarkably astute businessman. A serial entrepreneur, he made a fortune from the recruitment business SThree, which he set up and then floated in 2005, and today he remains a small shareholder of Tottenham Hotspur. From an Irish family, growing up in Tooting, he was one of only a few people at his school to get to university: Bill studied at the London School of Economics. A natural and gifted entrepreneur, a great people manager and motivator, a superb salesman and tough minded in a business sense. His first-ever business venture was when he was eight years old at the time of decimalisation. (The British pound was made up of 20 shillings, each of which contained 12 pence. On 15 February 1971, the British currency was converted to the decimal system, with 100 pence to the pound.) He worked out that shops could make use of a chart on the wall showing what, for example, three old pence was in the new money. So he wrote it up as a diagram, got it printed and went round selling it to all the local shops. He sold his first print run and was about to order a second when he saw that the *Sun* newspaper had copied his idea and printed a similar chart as a centrefold giveaway, so he called it a day. Not a bad start to a career. Bill was a significant contributor to our success over the coming four years, in no small measure because his wily intelligence always kept me on my toes, and never let me get complacent about my position or my tactics.

Bill's shareholding was represented on the board by Ian Colletts, who managed Bill's family office investing.[14] A man of whom both I and my wife Em are immensely fond, a man whose family celebrations from bar mitzvahs to weddings we've had the pleasure of attending, Ian was nevertheless someone who concerned me when I first came on board. I didn't know if I could trust him – I didn't know if he was in effect a rogue operator reporting back to Bill. This was

---

14 A family office is the phrase used to denote the administrative set-up used by wealthy families to manage their financial investments.

probably down to the fact that he was the main person I'd been negotiating with on my contract, and my reticence as far as he was concerned was probably more to do with me protecting my position in those negotiations. Nothing could have been further from the truth: Ian became a wise and solid counsel for the entire period I was at Meantime, right up to the day of the sale itself. A devout believer in his faith, a real family man, he is someone I would trust wholeheartedly.

Tony Carson is the son of the comedian Frank Carson and grew up in Blackpool. He made his first fortune by building up the Taipan Taverns chain, which he sold to Noble House Leisure, and he has been a serial investor ever since. A soulful and intelligent man, he was of crucial help to me with support during the 2011 fundraise and in encouraging me to find more investors so that we wouldn't have to rely on the existing senior shareholders to support us. He'd come in to Meantime during Hooky's 2009 fundraise and had brought several of his contacts with him. I respect him immensely. When first his father and then two years later his mother died during the Meantime years, he asked me to sit and keep him company while he waited to hear the news, a role I considered an honour. Today, hearing my phone ring and seeing the name Tony Carson on it will inevitably bring a smile to my face.

Finally, I met up with Hooky and he and I thrashed out a working partnership which, to his immense credit, he never once in four years attempted to vary. As became our habit, we sorted most of this out on the golf course, but eventually we had a written job description and contract which gave me complete authority to run the company and enabled Hooky to maximise his creative skills as head brewer. He made it clear that he didn't see himself as a CEO and he welcomed me taking the role on, leaving him much freer to focus on what he knew best. With that sorted, I was free to tell SAB Miller that I was leaving and, after a month or two's gardening leave over the summer, allowing me to take the family off for some well-deserved holiday time, I walked into Meantime that September morning in 2011.

My job was to turn Meantime into the genuine consumer success which my team and I had identified as being possible a year before. What was holding it back? Why, after ten years of operations and 18 months after a successful £3.4 million fundraise, did the business only turn over £4.5 million in 2010 and make a loss of more than £600,000? Well, some of that loss, about £150,000, could be accounted for by the move to the new premises in Blackwall Lane but still there was every reason for the senior shareholders to feel nervous about the direction of travel.

As I've already mentioned, the problem didn't lie in the quality of the people; that first week in September 2011, I had one-to-ones with all the key staff and I was impressed by the dedication, the spirit, the experience, the skills. These were for the most part talented, self-starting individuals who loved the brand they worked for. You just needed to walk around the huge, glistening steel tanks on the brewery floor to get a sense of commitment, camaraderie and a can-do attitude. Businesses the size of Meantime as it was then can exude a real sense of muscle which can outweigh the actual financial performance, and I knew that I'd come to work with some people who I'd be honoured to lead.

So the people were, on the whole, really impressive; the kit wasn't bad either. Hooky had used a big chunk of his £3.4 million fundraise to buy the best and the biggest brewing tanks he could afford. They shone in the Greenwich sunlight, massive steel installations which in all honesty were a lot bigger than Meantime had required back in 2009. In fact, by the time we came to sell the business in 2015, we were still not using those massive tanks to their full capacity. So you could say that Hooky had over-ordered back in 2009, had given rein to his brewer's enthusiasms to buy the best tanks he could without really calculating whether he needed such volume. But as usual, there are two sides to every story: when I did come to sell the business in 2015, one of the factors I folded into the price ticket was the fact that the purchaser would already have the kit in place to upscale production massively. Swings and roundabouts: Hooky had really made the right decision back then, even if his cash flow didn't necessarily support it, because the size of your boil kettle is crucial to your growth. You can always add more maturation tanks, but if your boil kettle isn't big enough to service them, you can't build quantity.

Despite the fact that the massive, shiny tanks turned out several years later to be a strategic plus, when I came on the scene in 2011 they were acting more like heavy weights dragging behind the boat. The company had spent so much money on them, and because it wasn't remotely aggressive enough in its overall sales philosophy, it didn't ever have enough cash in the business. (Aggression in sales is a good thing as long as it's delivered with a smile and a retailer benefit.) This had led Hooky and the board to make a couple of decisions in the years leading up to my arrival which were strategically extremely unsound for the longer term.

The first was an agreement made with Adnams in 2008

to give them the right to distribute Meantime beer from our brewery and brew cask ale at their own brewery in Suffolk under the Meantime name and distribute it around the country. Effectively, Adnams were running the on-trade outside London for Meantime. The Meantime board's rationale back in 2008 had probably gone something like this: we don't have enough cash in the business to push our brand outside London so Adnams can do a bit of that for us, plus we'll make a bit of cash as they make sales for us. It was all done on a fairly ad hoc, gentlemanly basis – the beer industry is very capable of operating in an honourable way in that fashion and always has done. You help me out here, we'll both benefit. The big problem with this – and there were others, but this was the biggest – is that salesmen, on the whole, tend to sell the product in their portfolio which is easiest for them to sell or earn the most money on. That's just human nature. And Meantime in 2008–2011 wasn't well known outside of London, so the Adnams salespeople were always going to have an uphill struggle selling the beer into the trade, just like I struggled in 1986 to sell Carling in an East End which had grown used to Fosters. So while it sounded a useful agreement in theory, in practice it wasn't delivering the goods. The Meantime cask ale that Adnams were brewing under the terms of this agreement was effectively being sold, or attempting to be sold, into free houses as a 'guest beer' alongside the primary Adnams range. And of course, 19 times out of 20, the free houses were sticking with the Adnams they knew.

Almost the first decision I took that first week in September was to tell Hooky that I planned to cancel the Adnams agreement. Everything was wrong about it: it would constrain our ability to build our own sales operation, and by allowing Adnams to brew a Meantime cask ale, we were contradicting our own brand proposition. You're either a cask beer brand sitting alongside warm-served pub cask brands or you're a craft ale being delivered chilled with a distinctive, fresh, carbonated, hoppy flavour; you can't be both. Even though the Adnams agreement, flawed though it was, was delivering a thousand hectolitres of sales every year to Meantime and was creating some additional capacity in the limited numbers of bottles we were selling through them, it was far more damaging strategically than it was positive in cash terms. The negative impact on the Meantime brand was more significant than the fact that it enabled us to fill up a bit more space in those big shiny tanks as we shipped bottles out to Adnams; plus the small amount of income we were getting from the cask ale which Adnams were brewing under our name was, looked at strategically, negligible. If you look at the agreement from the other side, Adnams had no such brand concerns because they knew their brand was admired and respected throughout the country; being associated with Meantime wouldn't impact on their customers or consumers one iota. Plus, they got a bit of overhead recovery.[15] From their perspective, not a bad call.

I knew their managing director Andy Wood (originally a Greenwich lad) and the chairman Jonathan Adnam very well from previous stages in my career. Jonathan was a particularly interesting character: you could be having a meeting with him in their Suffolk HQ when his bleeper would go off and he'd run out of the room. As well as being

15 Overhead recovery is the amount of overhead recovered in relation to the direct costs of production.

chairman of Adnams, he was a volunteer lifeboatman for the RNLI. Adnams were – they still are – a company made up of decent, honourable, successful people and it wasn't a problem for me to have an open conversation with them. I explained that I had plans to build Meantime and that the Adnams relationship would hold me back; they understood completely, we shook hands and the deal was ended.

The second difficult decision undertaken by the Meantime board before my arrival was to enter into a contract brewing deal with what was in effect a rival craft beer company. Brewing for them in theory got cash into the business and used up some of that spare capacity. The problem was, the rival was BrewDog, who were clearly outgunning us from a marketing perspective. The agreement was signed in the Spring of 2011, at a period when BrewDog were building a big new brewing facility of their own but needed some extra capacity while they did so. When I arrived that September, I found that we were brewing up to 5000 hectolitres[16] of beer for BrewDog at our own premises and our payment terms were, putting it politely, not particularly advantageous to us. I realised immediately that the commitment to make so much beer for BrewDog was limiting our ability to service our own orders: those shiny tanks should have been making Meantime, not BrewDog. Not only that, but the contract brewing agreement had been drafted in what was in my opinion a far too nebulous manner, such that there wasn't sufficient clarity on the exact quality and character of the beer to be delivered. One of the many challenges in brewing unpasteurised, partially filtered beer (which were the charac-

---

16 Alcohol is typically measured in hectolitres – one hectolitre is 100 litres (about 176 pints).

teristics of both BrewDog and Meantime craft beers) is that the final product is susceptible to slight changes in character. That's partly what makes craft ale so attractive: it's got real personality. But the very fact of this created an ambiguity in the contract between Meantime and BrewDog which was bound to lead to problems.

BrewDog had been founded in Scotland in 2007 by James Watt and Martin Dickie on the back of a phenomenal crowdfunding strategy and a marketing profile which gave them clout on the street: they were the beer punks and they called their bestselling beer Punk IPA. James Watt in particular made a massive noise about how they were the anarchist punks trying to scale the walls of the corrupt old corporate beer industry, the conglomerates. BrewDog told the world they hated the big beer companies and I arrived at Meantime on the back of five years at one of the world's biggest brewers, SAB, selling Peroni lager. I was the devil incarnate. It was an interesting contrast: BrewDog had without a doubt done a fantastic job in creating such a powerful brand from scratch and building it with authenticity and passion. At Miller Brands, we'd taken an existing brand, Peroni, and transformed it using an unwavering strategic discipline.

I had my first meeting with James on my third day, 14 September 2011, and it was, shall I say, frosty. I like to think that I stayed polite, probably thinking in the back of my mind that I'd actually *been* to Sex Pistols and Clash gigs. The contract stumbled on for a further 12 months before we finally managed to negotiate a cancellation and for all that time there was an acrimonious smell to the relationship throughout. We were constantly sparring with each other about all sorts of issues, and it didn't make for a happy marriage. Then, early in 2012, they came to the table to agree to terminate the brewing contract with Meantime. In retrospect, I suspect both of us knew that the kitchen was going to be a little too hot to work together; we were, after all, rivals within a precise market sector, craft beer.

What both the Adnams and BrewDog contracts demonstrated was the weakness in Meantime's situation in 2011. Each contract had been entered into to tackle a shortfall in cash which in turn would have been down to over-expenditure on equipment and underperformance in sales. It had become a Catch-22 problem for the board: they couldn't sell more beer because their brewing capacity was being taken up by rival brands; but they couldn't get out of those contracts because their sales operation wasn't strong enough to deliver the cash the business needed. In every single business in the world, cash is king, and at Meantime, the king wore no clothes.

What a working career teaches you, though, is that the answer to the problem is never straightforward. There are always multiple causes for any one given business effect and, remember, I was coming into this business in September 2011 having had the luxury of utilising SAB's firepower to produce an incredibly detailed report which had proved to me beyond doubt that Meantime had more potential than any other craft beer business in the country. For that reason, all the weaknesses which were holding the business back must, by definition, be capable of being tackled. What were they?

1. **Cash.** I've touched on cash. Meantime didn't have enough for me to be able to untap the potential of the business, so I knew before I arrived that we'd need to

raise more investment. The good news was we had a strong group of investors already; the bad news, that they had become unsettled. Throughout the entire time I led Meantime, I never went a day without worrying about cash.

2. **Discipline.** There was a lack of discipline in the business: there were too many 'meerkats', forever bobbing up and down, putting their heads up and making suggestions without seeing them within the context of a strategy. Despite being a congenitally headstrong lad, I'd learned over years at big companies that lack of discipline costs sales. It's not glamorous, it's not sexy, but building successful businesses requires absolute discipline. Remember what I said about the traits of successful business people? Eighty-five per cent of the decisions they take are taken with the business in mind, not their personal preference. I knew that we had to get people at Meantime to focus on the task they had been brought in to deliver.

3. **Focus.** Meantime was made up of largely excellent, likeable and diligent people, but they weren't focused on the goal. For a team to win, every member has to know, understand and commit to the goal, and comprehend their role within the team. In all honesty, the goal before my arrival had been perfectly sound in some respects: to make the best craft beer that they could. But that goal hadn't translated into sales and it was showing no signs of doing so. The business needed a much clearer focus on why it existed, and coming in as I did on the back of a shareholder request, it was

clear to me that the focus had to include achieving value for shareholders.

4. **Strategy**. There was no clear strategy coming from the top on what the company intended to do, what actions it planned to take over the next three to five years, where it intended to be. Without a strategy, you're a slave to events. I was a lot older and wiser than the lad who'd raced to open the shoe shop in Darlington after a night on the tiles and I had every intention of making strategy one of our core foundations at Meantime.

5. **Time**. The company didn't have much time. I could feel in my bones the level of nervousness felt by the senior shareholders who had invested significant sums two years before my arrival and had yet to see real results. The clock was ticking. Everyone loved Meantime but now too many people, from shareholders to trade journalists to our pub group customers, had an inkling that change and progress needed to be on the horizon.

6. **Energy**. There wasn't enough energy pumping through the company for my liking. It's one of the most misunderstood and neglected characteristics of successful businesses. If you follow a day in the life of almost every truly successful entrepreneur, the one thing you'll notice is: they never stop. They just never stop. The more energy you have, or you learn to conserve, then the more time and opportunity you're creating for your idea or your product to succeed. It's that simple, although the Dragons sitting in their elegant suits in languid poses on that TV programme

like to pretend otherwise. Don't let them fool you: each of them has more energy in one little finger than Winnie-the-Pooh's Tigger. Only they use it a bit more effectively.

There was a lot to do, but I'd come prepared and knew I was going to have to work harder than I'd ever done. I was expecting to find 'snags' like the Adnams and BrewDog deals and knew they could be dealt with, but it's the unexpected perils which can upset the best-laid plan. I was to find plenty of those in the coming months.

Chapter Four

'Hello Nicky!'

I don't mind admitting that during those first few weeks at Meantime, I had more than one sleepless night in the new flat I'd just taken a whopping mortgage out on. It wasn't the mortgage payments that kept me awake though – I'd decided on abandoning the security of the corporate world so I knew that personal financial risk came with that decision. No, what really gave me the jitters was that every time I lifted up a stone, I seemed to find something rather nasty underneath. I wasn't being deliberately provocative but I was going in pretty hard in September and October, demanding answers which sometimes ended up giving me the heebie-jeebies. That was another lesson I learned from sport, I suspect: make your first tackle count and let people know you're not a pushover. But with this approach, you have to be prepared to stand firm when you get a reaction.

At the age of 24, I learned some of these lessons when I was promoted to be an area manager for Bass. I'd spent my first two years at Bass working under Tony Baumann as a salesman. Tony is a top bloke, and still a great sharer of WhatsApp funnies. He was a bundle of nervous energy, always quick to respond, never afraid of getting up close and personal if he thought you weren't delivering. He reminded me of a powerful bloodhound and would always find his own solution to a problem, however unorthodox. His nickname was Ticker because in the early 80s, the days of IRA bomb threats in London, he'd come back to his car and heard a ticking noise from the boot. He called the bomb squad who evacuated the area, opened the boot and found Tony's alarm clock.

Tony drilled so many sales lessons into me during those two years. I remember him once sitting in the car after he'd joined me on a sales call, and he started waving his hands above his head.

'What are you doing?' I asked him.

'These are all the blooming buying signals which you just missed in that meeting,' he said, indicating them flying over my head. Tony and other inspiring teachers from that time drummed it into me just how crucial it is to identify the decision-maker in the organisation you're trying to sell to because otherwise you're literally wasting your time. You can have all your patter ready and finessed, but if you're trying to sell to the wrong person, then you're not going to make the sale.

Then in 1988, a Bass reorganisation saw Tony moved to run the central district, and he tried to lure me to join him with the offer of a £2,000 per annum pay rise. In those days, the working hours for a Bass salesman in the West End of London were 3 pm to 3 am because basically your job was to be in all the nightclubs selling the product. I was 23 at the time and the idea of being paid to be out in nightclubs in Soho every night seemed just too good to miss. But something – let's call it instinct – made me sit back and consider: was I really going to be doing myself a favour by pretending to be the King of Soho? Wasn't the risk of this that I'd enjoy it too much and become trapped in sales forever? So instead, I went to see the man who'd taken over the East region territory, another big influence on my career, who you could easily predict would become very senior in the organisation: Peter Swinburn. Peter was smart, ambitious and competitive, and a very astute manager of people. He'd played on the wing for Wales as an under-19, was a dab hand with a fly fishing rod and managed to make wearing a beige suit seem effortlessly cool.

'I understand Tony's trying to make you move to Central,' he said.

'He is.'

'And are you going?'

'Not if we can agree this,' I said. 'If you can match his £2,000 pay rise offer, and give me £5,000 of advertising and promotions money, then I reckon I can deliver you a thousand barrels[17] of incremental beer sales in the working men's clubs of Dagenham in the next year. And if I deliver you that, you'll get me promoted into Bass Taverns with an area of managed houses to run.'

Peter thought about it – I think he admired my cheek – looked at me, then nodded his head. I delivered him his thousand barrels of sales in seven months and, good as his word, he organised for me to gain promotion in 1990 to run

---

17 One barrel contained 288 pints, which meant that I was claiming I could create an additional sale of 288,000 pints of beer.

18 pubs in north-east London. The actual interview for the move from Bass Brewers into Bass Taverns was a classic. I was playing a cricket match for Bass against one of the other brewers, and we were playing in the august surroundings of Churchill College in Cambridge. It was a glorious day, and I'd managed to convince our captain that I was a batsman, even though I was actually primarily a bowler, so I was put in at number four. We lost two wickets early on so I was in, batting with the regional boss of Bass Taverns, David Henderson, the first time I'd met him. David is a Scot and a passionate Rangers fan, as competitive as me when it came to both sport and business. He was a wiry, tough little fellow, always cheerful, empathetic and a fantastic manager of people. Over the next two hours, he and I shared a partnership to score 200 runs, and as we passed each other on the crease and gathered briefly at the end of each over, he casually interviewed me about my suitability for running a group of pubs. A week later, I heard I'd got the job.

I'd moved on from sales into retail and a whole new learning experience; Peter Swinburn, to his endless credit, went on later in his career to run Coors Worldwide, one of the biggest jobs in global beer. And once the news of Meantime's sale had gone public in 2015, he took me out to lunch.

'Well done, Miller,' he said. 'I've got to tell you, I didn't see that coming.'

Thirty years before, if I'd fallen for the lure of Soho nights, I'd never have moved out of sales, I'd never have broadened my skills and, ultimately, would never have found myself getting the opportunity to run Meantime. It was a big decision, one of those very few massive life decisions which, when you're young, you sometimes don't fully recognise for the impact they are going to make on your life. When you make those big calls, and you call them right, you open up an entirely new and much broader horizon for your career. Some call it luck, some call it following your instinct, but whatever you call it, you must be brave in the decisions you take. This idea of sacrificing short-term gains for a long-term objective is obviously a core component of strategic planning, useful in considering your own life and career as well as planning the trajectory of a company or brand.

So there I found myself, at the age of 24, in charge of 18 Bass pubs in north-east London. I'd learned a lot about sales; I'd worked out that the harder I worked the more sales I made, and I'd discovered or been taught many of the scams which buyers can try and pull on the unwary salesman. To prepare me, David Henderson had sent me to do six months of stocktaking in East End pubs, telling me wisely that unless I understood how the industry added up the numbers, there would be no way I could manage a pub. I was fortunate also, because my brother Peter came to live with me in a little two-up, two-down house in Leytonstone which I bought, and it was great to be able to kick back with my brother at the end of another long day, chew the fat, talk nonsense as usual. Peter decided he was going to move to Australia and left in 1993; with hindsight, it was a particular pleasure to be able to spend time with him. He's been in Australia ever since, married to another Emma and with two delightful children, Harry and Georgina. Peter and I like to visit each other as much as we can these days.

The late 80s was dominated by the impact of AIDS and a few Bass Charrington pubs in London had a predominantly gay customer base. Just before taking up the retail role, while still a stocktaker, I'd gone to check on the stocks at a pub in St Katharine's Dock called the Ivories, and found the landlord dead in his bed, killed by that terrible disease. As an industry, we had to take on that threat and all the official government advice at that time encouraged us to introduce new levels of cleanliness and sanitation to protect our staff and customers, a foretaste of what was to come with the Covid-19 pandemic.

At another pub I managed, the Bell in Kings Cross, the main entertainment was the fairly edgy late-night drag evenings with male burlesque performers dressed as glamour girls. It was a popular gay venue and the door was managed by a series of black belt-qualified women, hard-as-nails lesbians. Their boss was a woman called Chris who was quite famous in London in the 80s and I got to know and like her quickly. The manager of the pub was a big six-foot-two fella whose partner was sadly dying from AIDS, and who I'd had to retire the previous week because of his terminal health. The pub itself I was wary of; the place always felt to me like there wasn't something quite right going on. One day, I got a phone call from Chris:

'Nick, I'm ringing to complain about this franchise fee I'm paying. You've raised it to £1100 and it's too much.' The franchise fee was what she paid for managing the door and the ticket sales she and her team got for the acts they put on in the pub. You needed really good people like Chris and her women to control drugs going into your venues; they ran the whole entertainment and security brilliantly. Something about what she said immediately didn't smell right to me and I looked at what we called our weekly statement of business and realised something was wrong.

'Chris, you'd better come and talk to me.'

When she arrived, I said:

'Chris, how long have you been paying this £1100?'

'Well, I've been paying £1000 for three years and two weeks ago you lot put it up to £1100. It's too much; I can't make any money.'

I showed her my sheet.

'Chris, the weekly statement says you've been paying £600 a week for the last three years. We've got a problem, haven't we? We're going to have to pull the manager in.'

I went to see my boss, David Henderson, and he pulled the landlord in for a three-hour disciplinary hearing with full security. Chris gave evidence. The landlord was sacked for ripping her and us off by £500 a week. Chris was terrified all this time; she was convinced the landlord, now sacked from his job, would come for her. An hour after the hearing, I took Chris down to the foyer of the Charrington's building where the tribunal had been held to see her out. As soon as I reached the ground floor, the landlord burst through the front door and began to run at me. He was a big chap, he was furious, he'd just lost his partner to AIDS, and we'd just fired him. For ten minutes, he chased me around the Charrington's foyer like a scene from the Keystone Cops, shouting and swearing, until I exhausted him by keeping ahead of him and security managed to eject him.

I said to our security team that we'd better go in and check the pub out. The first thing we found when we went in was an empty coffin in the cellar. Upstairs, we discovered a fully fledged S&M torture chamber with racks of whips, a rubber suit hanging off the ceiling and one of those school gymnastic pommel horses complete with shackles. There was also the inevitable spare, unauthorised till. Word got around because miraculously, overnight, the pub was broken into and all the torture equipment was stolen. Heaven knows where it was installed next but we breathed a sigh of relief to see it disappear from our managed house.

With this sizeable chunk of retail estate to manage, I was really going to begin to learn some lessons about human nature and how to deal with adversity. The six months of stocktaking had taught me that you had to view the books of a pub with a healthy dose of scepticism. 'Buying out' was endemic: the trick whereby pub managers would buy their own bottles of whisky, keep the profit to themselves and try and fool the stocktaker by fiddling the till reports. Although the arrival of computerised EPOS[18] systems in the 90s made that kind of game harder, it was eye-opening to see how inventive pub managers would be to pull the wool over your eyes.

But at the same time, once I became the area manager of these 18 pubs, I began to learn that it wasn't always in my interest to catch the managers out. Pubs in north-east London in the 80s and 90s were pretty tough places – protection rackets, gangsters, IRA sympathisers, fences – and sometimes, when you knew a landlord was skimming a bit of his profit for himself but was keeping all the local hoodlums under control, you thought: I think I'll let him keep his unapproved bonus; he's worth it. We had pubs all along the Holloway Road in North London, and some were IRA pubs while others were Protestant. I had absolutely no knowledge or idea about the realities of these sectarian

18 EPOS, electronic point of sale, effectively computerised all sales transactions in environments like pubs and clubs.

divides. One of the managers was an ex-IRA official and one day, in drink, he walked over the road to another of our pubs which was run by an ex-RUC policeman. The IRA fellow picked an argument with a deputy manager, then punched him. I had to discipline him and at the hearing, sober now, he begged me not to fire him. I agreed to go and negotiate with the ex-RUC manager to see if I could get him to drop the charges. He kept me waiting for 45 minutes, even though I was his area manager. Fuming, I let myself into the basement of his pub, checked his cash safe and discovered that he was £5000 down. It turned out he'd 'borrowed' the money to pay for a holiday and planned to pay it back later. So I suspended him on the spot and, while we found a replacement manager, I had to run the pub for three days with all his pro-RUC customers hurling abuse at me and some relieving themselves against the bar. I'm not religious myself but I do believe in fairness and this kind of hatred was new to me.

Now I was an area manager, I had my own stocktaker, a lovely young lad called Rupert: good looking, extremely posh, privately educated. One of my pubs was the Black Cap in Camden, which was a drag bar with a Tuesday night special: Regina Fong, in full regalia. When I'd turn up for an inspection, Reg would be sitting there in his dressing room with his tackle on display.

'Hello Nicky!' he'd shout, and wave his tackle at me.

'Put it away, Reg!' was my standard riposte. He was a kind, very funny man and I liked him a lot; he was a legend in that sector back then.

Once I started sending pretty young Rupert in to check the stock, he'd have his bottom pinched endlessly, never more so than at the pub I mentioned earlier, the Bell in Kings Cross. The Bell was now run by an outrageously funny fellow called Simon Catt, who'd taken over from the landlord we'd fired over the franchise racket. Simon liked to dress up in drag with a pointed metal bra. Rupert arrived to do the stocktake, opened the safe in the basement to count the cash, and found instead a live, seven-foot boa constrictor. He leapt up on to the desk and started screaming, while Simon ran around the room laughing. Eventually, Rupert managed to reach the telephone and rang me.

'Nick!' this very posh voice yelled. 'There's a bloody snake in the safe!'

I knew Simon and I liked him, and I could tell this was one of his pranks. So I just said:

'Well, you'd better get it out then,' and put the phone down.

Ten minutes later, the phone went again.

'Nick, the snake's still in the bloody safe! I can't count the cash!'

I told him to put Simon on the line.

'Simon,' I said. 'Is it funny?'

'Ooh, it's hilarious; he's terrified, the poor love.'

'Probably time to put the snake away, Simon,' I said.

'All right, I'll put him back in his cage.'

Five minutes later, the phone goes again.

'Nick! He hasn't put it back in its cage!'

'Put Simon on.'

Simon was still laughing when he picked up.

'Simon, if you don't put that bloody snake back in its cage, I'm going to go to B&Q and buy a shovel and come round and chop its bloody head off.'

Finally, the snake was put back to bed.

These were tough, raw, visceral places. You saw every kind of human being, every kind of behaviour. With some of the pubs I was managing, I'd make a point of not hanging around outside when it was dark. I was threatened on a regular basis, and even had to resort to chucking the odd drunk out when he came at me with a bottle. There were some pubs where, as soon as I walked in, all the lights would go on and the whole place would go silent until they realised I was from the brewery, not the police.

'It's all right lads,' someone would yell out, 'he's from the brewery.' And the lights would go back to normal and the conversation would renew.

We had a pub called the Turnpike run by a tough Northern Irish publican called Billy. One Friday evening, I was at home with the TV on and there was a news item about a shooting incident at a pub in north London called the Turnpike. Someone had been shot dead standing at the bar: apparently, two pimps had been arguing at the bar over a girl. The next morning, I went straight there and found Billy washing down the floor of the bar with antiseptic cleaner. The police had got all the information they needed and had given him leave to open up. I went up to him, all concerned.

'Billy, are you going to be all right? Are you sure you're OK to open up? We can provide some post-traumatic stress counselling, you know.'

'Ha, get away with you,' said Billy. 'I've seen much worse on the Shankhill Road. The knee-cappings there were much nastier; they'd howl like dogs. We'll be open at twelve.'

At the same time, it was a wonderful eye-opener to the wider world. There are some seriously impressive people now in the upper echelons of the UK beer industry who cut their teeth in Bass Taverns.

I remember once making a regular visit to a pub in Stoke Newington. The pub had been doing well in recent weeks. It had been a real rough joint before, fights every night, and we'd swapped the tables in the pool hall for snooker tables, hoping the more elegant game might encourage some better behaviour. Before long, the fights had calmed down and the takings were up.

I took a pint from the manager, who looked over at a table in the corner.

'Those four gents want a word with you,' he said.

I went over to sit at the table where the four fellows were. They were all at least 20 years older than me, and it was pretty obvious that they were all strangers to the concept of 'an honest day's work'.

'Nice to meet you gents,' I opened up.

'So you're pleased with the pub, I hear,' one of them said. 'You think your snooker tables sorted out the trouble?'

'Does seem to have quietened down, yes,' I said.

'Idiot,' he replied. 'You know why the fighting's stopped? Because we ordered it. And now we want you to pay us for our services. Every week.'

It was a classic protection approach, only for me, as a 25-year-old pub retail manager, it was a first.

'I can't do that,' I said. 'This is a Bass pub; there's no way I can authorise anything like that.'

The fellow leaned in to me, his broken nose inches from my face.

'Do you want this pub to be still here next week or not?'

I thought quickly. This was no joke. I had a pub to

manage, I was responsible for the staff, for the customers.

'Look,' I said. 'You know I can't authorise that. I'm not doing it. But can I just make one request: if anything does happen to this pub, can it please happen when there's no one in it?'

A week later, in the middle of the night, the pub was set on fire and never opened again; the police to my knowledge never found out who was responsible or what the cause was.

They were tough days but invaluable to me. The experience allowed me to move out of sales into the broader area of management. I learned to get along with every kind of person, and I learned not to discriminate against anyone: as long as you did your job and you fulfilled your potential, you should be treated well. The other crucial learning experience from this time was getting to understand profit and loss (P&L), taking full responsibility for money coming in and costs going out. I was responsible for the financial performance of 18 pubs and without having absolutely strict control over the figures, there's no way I would have been able to manage them.

The important thing was to understand what levers you could pull to make a difference to a pub's P&L. I called it the One Per Cent Rule, which worked like this:

- Say one of your pubs takes £10,000.

- It has a 50% margin, giving you a gross margin of £5,000.

- Then you've got operating costs: staff, heat, light, rent, rates. Normally these would account for roughly 25% of turnover, so you've got £2,500 of costs, leaving you £2,500 of net pre-tax profit.

- Now, if you increase your turnover by 1% to £10,100 – which you might do by putting up prices or by running a promotion to increase footfall – you're also going to increase margin by reducing waste or by negotiating prices better or by selling a more premium spirit with a higher price. So let's say your gross margin is now £5,151, which is 51% of £10,100.

- Next you reduce your costs by 1% to £2,475 by rotating staff better, by turning the lights off, by purchasing cleaning materials cheaper, and so on.

- £5,151 minus £2,475 leaves you a net pre-tax profit of £2,676, which is a 7% profit increase.

- So just by applying the 1% rule, you can increase profits by 7%.

It's a simple rule but it applies to every business in the world, and certainly applied when I came to be in charge of both Peroni and Meantime. You're aiming for rapid turnover growth while increasing your gross profit and controlling your costs – if you do that, then you get what's called overhead recovery (see also Chapter Three), a simple mathematical formula which will always enable you to maximise your profit. I learned the rule while managing the pubs in north-east London and I used it throughout my career. In fact, I'd even go so far as to say that your ability to be successful in a volume-based business depends on it.

That period of my life also gave me more life lessons about handling adversity, how not to back off from a challenge and how not to get thrown by the unexpected. And the unexpected started to come thick and fast at Meantime as soon as I joined, with a series of reminders, as though I needed them, that life in a small, independent brewery was going to be very, very different to the life I'd led up until then as a salaried PLC employee. There were no internal structures, no organisational planning, and the working environment was messy and often chaotic. There wasn't any money and it was obvious I wouldn't be able to afford to pay my own salary in the first couple of months.

I began to apply methodical systems. If we were going to sell this business in five years' time, we needed every part of running as smoothly as a Rolls-Royce. I wanted to know how much we were paying for our electricity and no one seemed able to give me an accurate figure. I was getting exasperated when, one day, I noticed a bloke wandering around the yard below our office with a clipboard and a uniform.

'What's that bloke doing in our yard?' I called out.

No one answered me. I was keeping so many plates spinning at that time, I just didn't want another issue, so I carried on:

'Well? Who the bloody hell is he?'

It turned out he was from an electricity company, and he was trying to find the electricity meter. The reason he couldn't find it, I later discovered, was that some bright spark had bricked it up behind a false wall during some renovations, so that an accurate reading couldn't be made and a final bill served. We paid it eventually.

I couldn't believe it. Remember, I was determined to turn this company into the most desirable craft beer business in the country. It had to be absolutely solid, and within weeks I'd discovered we were operating with the electricity meter hidden behind a false wall.

'It's like working with Bonnie and Clyde, you cowboys!' I yelled at no one in particular. In fact, this was the only time I shouted during my four years at the company, and the fact that I did shows me in retrospect how stressful an initiation I'd had.

I knew our financial problems were going to be sorted with a new fundraise, and I was spending much of my time then talking to the existing 40-odd shareholders and talking to people in the industry who I thought might be interested in taking a stake. We completed a business plan demonstrating the need to raise in the region of £2.5 million and the accountants signed off the plan as being compliant with the government's Enterprise Investment Scheme. I've mentioned this before (Chapter Two): as a scheme, it's invaluable to growth companies, as it gives investors significant tax breaks, but it does commit the company to an exit strategy, which suited us: I'd come into this business with a plan to sell it for £50m in five years.

Then in November, two months after my arrival, disaster: the accountants told me that the headcount at Meantime during that financial year had exceeded 100 because we'd had to count the staff at the two pubs we managed, and the existing headcount limit to qualify for EIS was 100. In other words, having gone through the entire process of creating a business plan and prospectus, securing almost £2m investment commitments from existing shareholders and people in the industry, we now discovered at the very last minute that Meantime no longer qualified as an EIS company. This was potentially a fatal blow: it could mean that the investors who we had lined up to take a stake would walk away if they couldn't get the tax breaks they had been promised. And if they walked away, the company could rapidly fall into insolvency. I'd been taking decisions based on the projected arrival of that new injection of capital – personnel decisions, cancelling the Adnams agreement, commissioning new marketing and design work – and now there was the genuine risk we wouldn't be able to pay for it.

I had spent those early weeks both getting to know the senior shareholders and also negotiating so that Bill Bottriell, the biggest, would never be able to have more than a 25 per cent stake in the company. Uppermost in my mind was the plan to sell the business in five years for £50m; to do that, I needed to ensure that our buyer would be comforted by the fact that no one individual controlled the company with a stake larger than 25 per cent, and Bill, to his immense credit, had agreed to those conditions. But at the same time, in order to provide security for the company going forward, he also had agreed to underwrite the entire raise. In his canny and intelligent way, he was in effect using reverse psychology on me, increasing the pressure on me to find the investment for our raise from new shareholders or risk him gaining a bigger stake in the business.

I came into the business under no illusions: I was working for the shareholders. As soon as any business owner brings in investors, he or she is no longer just working for themselves; now, you're also working for the people who have expressed belief in you by investing their own money. Sometimes business founders can struggle to come to terms with that but it's a hard truth: your responsibilities now don't just include you, your staff and your customers – you also owe allegiance and loyalty to your shareholders.

Now, with this sudden disaster of the discovery of the

EIS failure, I might have to allow Bill to take up the full allotment of shares, he would have emerged as the dominant shareholder and would therefore potentially compromise my ability to impose my own strategy. I'd carefully negotiated with him to restrict him to under £1 million of the new raise, and I had responded to his challenge by sourcing almost £2 million from the other existing shareholders and from new shareholders that I found. Now, with the prospect of EIS being taken away from us, the only way we could have a hope of keeping going would be by Bill effectively taking over control of the business. My whole strategy would be sunk before I could start. These corporate structure issues are absolutely vital in the life of any business and they elide into personal relationships: you have to respect the people you are working with, and I certainly respected Bill, both for all he'd achieved to date and for the practical and sensible way in which he went along with these often delicate negotiations. He was ably assisted by Ian Colletts, who effectively represented his interests on the board. I grew to know and like Ian enormously and often relied on his sound judgement in those early days. During this difficult early period in particular, he demonstrated that judgement and his ability to balance the needs of the company with the interests of his client, a careful approach he maintained meticulously throughout those four years.

This discovery in November 2011 was pretty terrifying but looking back now, I'm struck by the way all of us – board members and senior shareholders as well as Meantime staff – kept our focus, kept our nerve and ploughed ahead. The accountants eventually found the solution: they told me that the word was that the government was going to change the rules for the next financial year, extending the minimum headcount from 100 to 250. So if we could delay accepting the investments I'd sourced until 6 April 2012, and if the government did change the rules in that way, we'd be able to complete the fundraise. That was almost six months of nail-biting balancing of books, several months of me not being able to pay my own salary or that of Hooky or Ben, several months of the company teetering on the edge of cash flow failure; all this and me still needing to run two mortgages and keep my family going. But we made it: the government did change the rules, we were able to accept the investments in early April and therefore we remained a soundly structured company with no shareholder holding more than 25 per cent of the company. We'd extended our shareholder base up to 70 people, which was a really solid foundation for building the strategy. We now had the funds to do what we needed to do.

To say that period was stressful is very much an under-statement. I was wired; I was working 18 hours a day, trying to hold it all together. It was all such a long way away from corporate life. In my previous corporate role, running Peroni for SAB, if we ever had a cash flow problem, we just asked the parent company to sub us a few million while we pulled expected revenues in. Now, down here in Greenwich, there was no one to turn to when the cash register was empty.

Oh, apart from the bank manager. While trying to sort out the impending disaster of the EIS issue, I was presenting to our relationship manager at Meantime's existing bank a case for borrowing just shy of £800,000 in loans. At one point, our manager invited Hooky and me to meet him for a day out driving cars at Thruxton race circuit down in Wiltshire. It's the kind of thing that senior bank executives love. We went there, and I was surprised to see our manager turn up in a brand new Aston Martin. Very nice, I thought. Only, it was a bit too nice, and very soon after – before he'd agreed to extend our loan or to approve the asset finance programme we'd presented to them – he disappeared without a trace. We never heard from him again, and the bank put a sudden halt on all projects he had been concerned with. We only found out what had happened a couple of years later, when Hooky was up for jury service and found out that the fellow had been arrested for fraud and ended up in prison. Unbelievable. It turned out he'd been fraudulent in some way, hence the flash Aston Martin.

Again, we solved this problem, in this case by moving to HSBC, after presenting to them a really thorough case for a combination of loan and asset financing which the whole senior team at Meantime threw themselves into, and in due course HSBC agreed £800,000 in loans and asset finance which, together with the eventual arrival of the £2.5 million in new investment, ensured that I could commit to the expansion strategy I'd had in my mind for a year. HSBC turned out to be a faultless banking partner, and as time went on it was a blessing that we'd been forced into moving to them. Their key people on our account – Amanda Murphy, Carol Bagnell, Sam Barker, Claire, Ian Tandy – were brilliant supporters of our business throughout. They would invite me to the occasional Friday evening dinners they held in Pall Mall, giving me the opportunity to present the Meantime vision to stakeholders, media and other key contacts. I also learned from the similar businesses who were invited to those evenings, among them Tangle Tease, Leon, Brompton Bicycles and Joseph Joseph.

But as you can see, the first few months threw terrific googlies down the pitch at me and I know that, without some of those earlier life experiences of learning to deal with adversity, just one of those googlies could have knocked us out. (A googly, or 'wrong 'un', is a cricket delivery which looks like a normal leg-spinner but actually turns towards the batsmen rather than away from the bat. Unlike a normal leg-break, a googly is delivered out of the back of the hand, with the wrist 180 degrees to the ground.)

The strange thing is, while we were all engaged in this incredibly pressurised settling-in period during those first six months, we also managed to build the bonds which keep most of us together to this day. Maybe that's it, maybe the adversity did bring us together quicker. I remember one evening, sitting at my wallpaper-pasting table which served as my desk, and Ben Joseph and his brother Dan came in. Their dad had just died, a charismatic and powerful fellow who'd been a professional gambler. At the end of one working day, the two of them went off to the gents and emerged dressed in black and both with balaclavas. I asked them what on earth they were doing hiding behind those. They explained that their dad's favourite spot had been the garden of the house he'd owned 20 years before: he'd loved to sit there with his copy of the *Racing Post*, a bottle of wine and his packet of Hamlet cigars. Their dad had been a proper character, given honourable mention in Mike Atherton's book *Gambling, A Story of Triumph and Disaster*. To honour his memory, they'd decided to spread his ashes in that garden, which was going to mean climbing over the wall in the middle of the night because the house was now owned by someone else. So the two of them, two middle-aged men, went out in the middle of the night to honour their dad in the way they felt he would have liked. It was this genuine sense of camaraderie which I felt very early on at Meantime, which sustained me through the relentless pressure and often loneliness of being in charge, and which I still relish to this day.

As I look back on my diary now from that period, despite the phenomenal stress levels caused by some of these unexpected pitfalls, I realise that I'd hurled myself into the business to such an extent that I was out almost every night of the week, and almost every one of those evening sessions was work: meeting up with potential investors, speaking to local Greenwich councillors or politicians, briefing old customers like Young's or Waitrose about my plans for the Meantime brand. I organised everything myself – no secretary, just an old pocket Letts diary which I'm looking at now – and once a week, before I headed back to Newbury to spend the weekend with the family, I'd strip down to my boxer shorts, crank up the Clash tracklist playing on the CD and I'd clean my new flat in Greenwich so that it would be ready for me, spick and span, on Monday morning.

I'd come to Meantime to make a difference. I wanted us all to win.

Chapter Five

People Have the Power

The people who worked at Meantime were as important as the ingredients Hooky used in brewing the beer. Some were classic south Londoners, full of street wisdom, wit and work ethic; others came from other parts of the country, other parts of the world, but all of them had that Meantime spirit of adventure, camaraderie and that crucial habit of looking out for each other. They were a family as much as a team and the whole business was built on that ethic. So, despite the fact that systems and methods didn't really exist outside of the brew itself, the business mainly kept going because of its internal spirit.

That's something I didn't want to tamper with, obviously. I was conscious of coming into this small, battling brewery from a very different background: a pretty high-end corporate environment, taking multi-million-pound decisions, with teams of people working for me across sales, finance, marketing, logistics. The last thing I wanted was for people at Meantime to see me as in any way either standoffish or remote, which was why I was really perfectly happy with my wallpaper-pasting desk. I deliberately didn't use any kind of MBA corporate-speak: no 'deep dives' or 'process re-engineering' nonsense. In a previous job I'd played 'buzzword bingo' with a colleague, which entertained us by letting us score points for spotting meaningless jargon being used in the workplace. At the same time, I could see there was a need to encourage better internal communications: it was obvious that people from different areas of the business could clash easily when there was no overall strategic lead. Therefore one initiative I brought in straight away was the 'town hall': every couple of weeks or so, the whole company would be encouraged to gather together for an hour and talk openly about the strategic plan, the current performance, and to vocalise any gripes and above all celebrate individual and team success. I asked different people to present each time so that everyone had a chance to take the floor. It became an engaging, informal but very useful way of binding us all in to one mission, so that we were all focused on growing the business out of the doldrums which had been threatening it.

We began to put a couple of hundred quid behind the bar of The Union in Greenwich, the pub we ran under our name, every Friday night so that Meantime employees could gather together and enjoy a social. It was a nice way of rounding off another demanding week and a good means of expressing the inclusive nature of the company: it was a chance for everyone to talk with each other, no matter what their role in the company. This became more important when I moved the 'office' staff – the management team, sales and marketing – out of the brewery building in Blackwall Lane and into an office set-up about half a mile away in the middle of Greenwich. I had to do that in order to clear space in the brewery building to expand capacity and bring on planned improvements like a visitor centre and bar, but I was aware it carried a risk of 'us and them' so I made sure that we kept up with the regular socials and town hall get-togethers.

When I came across a problem that could be solved in a collaborative way, rather than me coming over as the 'top-heavy' boss, then that's how we tackled it. It was obvious, for example, that there was a bit of 'leakage' from the brewery: beer unaccounted for, going missing. That just happens in life, it's human nature: they won't miss that box of beer – I'll pop that in the back of my car. We dealt with that in a very unconfrontational way, introducing much stricter product numbering and stock control, while at the same time having a pallet in the corner of the brewery where bottles that weren't quite right or in which the beer volume was slightly out, meaning we couldn't put them into the commercial system, were left for anyone to take for free. Even my son Sam took advantage of that when he came to work for us on the bottling line: you could hear the bottles clanking in his rucksack as he headed off home! Overall, it was a good way to keep the staff feeling they were being considered.

In strategic terms, this approach to working with your colleagues comes under the umbrella of the phrase popularised by American military computer expert Grace Hopper: 'Ask for forgiveness, not permission.' Hopper was a remarkable leader, rising to become a rear admiral in the US Navy on the back of her work in developing the use of computers in the military: Amazing Grace was her nickname. The phrase makes sense within the context of a skilled and motivated workforce: if you encourage good people to feel that they can make decisions without necessarily waiting for permission, you foster an incredible team spirit and desire for success. It is less useful when your colleagues are not up to scratch because obviously then they may get into the habit of taking bad decisions too often. At Meantime, this was never an issue: our people wanted to play at the top of their game, were accepting of change and desired to make a difference. Generally, they knew what to ask for and what not to.

As I'd progressed at Bass, I'd begun to absorb deep and lasting lessons about people, how to manage them, how to bring out the best in them. Bear in mind I was starting from quite a low level. Once, when I was running the Barratts shoe shop in Darlington, I'd fired a Saturday girl because our takings were down and we needed to cut costs. Instead of gently explaining this to her, this 19-year-old oik told her that she wasn't good enough. The next day, her mother came round to the shop and, quite rightly, slapped me in the face. These were learning experiences, even if it took a while for me to absorb the lesson: always focus on developing your empathy skills because good leadership simply isn't achievable without the humility that comes with setting aside your ego to work out what is driving the other person.

Once my stint running the 18 pubs in north-east London came to an end, Peter Swinburn, the smart operator who'd given me the opportunity to move out of sales, decided that my next move should be training people. That's what it's like, building a career inside a large organisation like Bass: your career is a combination of what you want, what you can do and, crucially, what your seniors decide is best for you and for the company. It's a complex series of relationships and impressions which, if you're lucky, end up with you building a strong portfolio of business skills; if you're unlucky, you can end up in a blind alley. My colleagues at Meantime – Hooky, with his gourmet's taste in life; Ben, with his street life background – hadn't experienced anything like this carefully curated career path, which was partly why Meantime was a fabulous mess by the time I arrived. I'd spent deliberate portions of my career being given the chance to operate successfully in very different areas – sales, people management, marketing, business analysis and leadership, product development and launches, finance – and I'd been as diligent as I could be in trying to extract the most from each stage.

So when Peter Swinburn told me I could move to Newbury to become a sales training manager, I leapt at it. I knew I didn't want to spend the next few years skulking around the back lanes of pubs in north-east London trying to work out ways of boosting sales and reducing fights; I also knew that, at the age of 25 and with no A-levels or university degree, I would always be fighting for my corporate opportunities with one hand tied behind my back. Bass, like all major corporations in the 1980s and 1990s, looked more kindly on graduates and provided fast-stream training schemes for them to reach upper management levels quickly. Did I have a chip on my shoulder? Absolutely. But at the same time, it was a chip I knew I'd carefully placed there myself by listening to the Clash and going to parties on my illegal motorbike when I should have been studying at school for my exams. I had myself to blame; the truth sets you free.

The solution seemed obvious to me then. I'd been

working for Bass for five years, I'd learned a huge amount about sales, I'd developed pretty good people skills on a one-to-one basis, I'd taken on board some of the rudiments about finance: how to project sales, how to factor in debt and overhead. If I was going to push myself into the position where I could compete with people of my age who were being boosted up the ranks because they had a university degree, then I needed to broaden my knowledge and skills so that my employer, Bass, would have to take notice of me. If I was going to progress quickly, I needed to be tougher than the rest and better equipped. I wasn't so worried about the first one; the second needed work.

Peter Swinburn, not for the first time and not for the last, had intervened in my career at exactly the right moment. If I'm honest, I don't think he did so out of a belief that I could go far; I've already mentioned that, when the Meantime sale was announced, he had the good grace to tell me that he hadn't expected me to achieve so much. Peter, like many managers, can see the strengths you currently have; the boss who sees what you could achieve with the right encouragement is much rarer. Even so, he did me an enormous favour by bringing me in as a sales trainer. He'd pulled me out of the rough and tumble of running pubs into the more rarified atmosphere of training people. And I was training graduates too: one of the Bass graduate trainees I began to tutor in class on closing techniques and the careful stages of conducting a sale was one Emma, now my gorgeous wife. It took us 20 years and the ending of both our first marriages to finally bring us together, and that's another 'thank you' I have to add to my list for Peter Swinburn!

My move to Newbury, to a new job as a training

manager, coincided with changes in both my own life and in the broader world of beer and pubs. I first married in 1991 and two years later our first child, Annie, was born. So home life was now very different, intense with emotion as all new parents will know. Meanwhile, around me, the business I'd spent the last five years in was being completely transformed. The government's Monopolies and Mergers Commission had concluded that the ownership of Britain's pubs, together with the beer they served, by just six big groups was not sustainable and with 1989's Beer Orders the Big Six were instructed to dismantle their operations. Bass split itself into two separate companies, with brewing in one and pub management in the other, and began the process of selling the assets in both, which it needed to do in order to comply with the government's decision. This was the moment when a brand like Meantime was able to become a possibility. It was the moment when smaller pub chains like Enterprise Inns and Punch Taverns began to emerge by strategically acquiring pubs that the Big Six were obliged to sell off; independent free houses became more common and drinkers began to be offered a broader choice of venue and tipple.

Bass's decision to set up what was effectively an in-company 'training university' was smart. Going forwards, the world for companies like Bass was going to be more competitive with so many new operators flooding onto the market. Gone were the days when a salesman like me might struggle in the East End just because it was Scottish & Newcastle territory; now, it was a free-for-all. So I was allocated six regional trainers reporting to me for the South of England, and I also took on the responsibility of training incoming Bass salespeople with a view to getting them operational as quickly as possible. My team and I were building training courses not just in the essentials of sales, but also specific courses in negotiation, finance, time management. Debbie Couzens worked in my team and actually wrote most of those courses. Debbie had forged her own career in the Welsh beer market so there wasn't much that could either surprise or intimidate her. She has four lovely daughters and a fine fellow of a man called Martin as her husband, who became a firm friend too. Debbie had the brains and the application to compile most of the training courses we needed to apply. My immediate boss, Brian Blake, who reported to Swinburn and was another massive influence on my career, took me by the scruff of the neck and told me in no uncertain terms that he was going to 'kick the absolute shit out of me'. What he meant was, I'd spent the last few years on the streets of East London, watching out for myself; now, I was in head office and I was going to have to learn how to navigate my way through the rapids of corporate life. Brian took no prisoners: sometimes, when I was sitting at my desk, he'd bang on the adjoining wall and yell, 'Miller, get in here!' I'd duly get up and walk into his office to find him scratching his head over the newspaper crossword. 'Three down, Miller. I can't get it. Have a go.' I'd shake my head and go back to my office. Much against my own instincts – because I've always hated the politicking that goes on inside the corporate world – I was going to have to learn how to manage some of those political games, and having the cigar-smoking legend that was Brian Blake to teach me was, in retrospect, no bad thing.

I threw myself into it. I went on every single Bass training course at least three times, both as part of my job as training manager, but also in my own mind as a way of broadening out my skill sets. I deliberately developed a skill which I'd begun to learn as a salesman on the streets of East London: how to listen and how to value listening. The ability to listen, not just with your ears but also with your eyes, is supremely important in business. Tony Baumann taught me that early on – 'Two ears, two eyes, one mouth: proportionate use, Miller!' – but now I was involved in training others I really began to understand the value of listening as a means of bringing out the best in people. Listening isn't just about hearing words; it's also about understanding body language, watching eye movements. We communicate with each other in a remarkably complex way and speech is just one component.

I began to learn too about questioning. If you ask people a direct question, they will normally answer you as best as they can. If they're trying to pull the wool over your eyes, then the funnel approach to direct questions I mentioned earlier (Chapter Two) will eventually trip them up. Dale Carnegie in his 1936 classic book *How to Win Friends and Influence People* suggested: 'Be a good listener. Ask questions the other person will enjoy answering.' By asking questions, as Alison Wood Brooks and Leslie K. John have set out in the *Harvard Business Review* (2018), we unlock value in organisations by spurring learning and the exchange of ideas, which then fuels innovation and performance improvement and builds trust and rapport between team members. I can't think of a single one of my bosses over the years who had a beneficial impact on my career who didn't ask more questions than they made statements. It's a habit ingrained in good leaders.

Listening and questioning are the polar opposites of stating and insisting. When you listen and question, you receive the information you need to make a business assessment in the shortest space of time; when you state and insist, you find out nothing. When I came to Meantime in 2011, I could have just stated to the 100-odd staff that I'd arrived with a mission to turn the business round and I could have insisted they did what I said. If I'd taken that approach, I wouldn't have found out where the critical issues in the business were quickly enough to be able to deal with them and I would also have lost the hearts and minds of the team. They would have dismissed me as a bumptious corporate oaf and would have begun to engage in either conscious or subconscious acts of rebellion. Of all the great bosses I've had the luck to work for in a 30-year career in the industry, not one of them failed that crucial test: they all listened and questioned before they made their minds up. Sometimes their decisions went against what I wanted but then maybe my pitch was wrong, or I didn't appreciate or agree with their needs.

If this sounds simplistic, then think again. Listening can often result in you having to let someone drone on for quite a while until they actually get to the point. But if you don't listen, if you don't put yourself through the droning, they'll spot that, and they'll see that you're not really listening at all: you're just pretending. Subsequently they'll start to clam up and you've lost your chance to find out the information you need to make the correct decision. In truth, you have to enjoy engaging with people, you have to see it as a human priority to allow the other person to express themselves, even if you'd prefer it if they expressed themselves a bit more quickly!

The first six months at Meantime, setting aside the

financial issues and the strategic planning, were all about listening to the people and working out where there were gaps and where we needed to supplement the team. There's a simple, crude technique for analysing team members which I learned in those early days at Bass Training. Once you've let people tell you how they operate, how they see the world, and you've had an opportunity to watch them in action, you can usually place them somewhere on a graph that looks a bit like this:

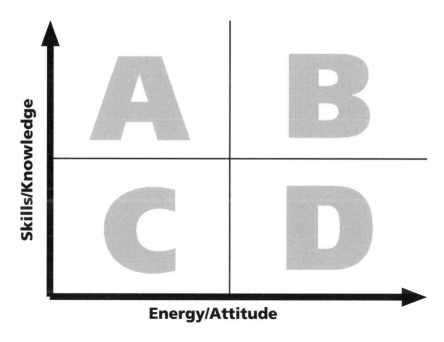

The most effective people in your team are probably in the top right B quadrant: they're full of energy and they know what they're doing. You're going to be confident in delegating responsibility to those colleagues. The ones who fall into the bottom right D quadrant are full of potential because they've got energy and the right attitude; they just lack skills, so the thing you do with them is to give them training. The people in the top left A quadrant need to respond to your motivation because they've got the skills but they haven't got the right attitude; you can manage and motivate them, and you may need to sell to them to get the best out of them. Those who fall into the bottom left C quadrant, with few skills and not a very good attitude, are going to need a lot of instruction from you; you effectively just have to tell them what to do. (There's also the extreme character who scores hugely on the bottom line but barely registers on the left-hand vertical; these people are terrorists, dangerous to your organisation with lots of negative energy and poor skills, and need to be weeded out.)

The people at Meantime, in general, when I first encountered them all, tended to do well along the horizontal line (energy/attitude) but, setting aside the specialist brewing skills which were obviously well established in the business, the upward line showing skills and/or knowledge was more patchy. We didn't have enough sales, marketing, finance, human resources or logistics skills in the business and those missing elements were going to seriously hold us back. I decided to adopt a mixed approach to that problem, combining the introduction of training with some judicious reallocation of roles and, crucially, some new appointments. If I'd had all the time in the world and had no financial ticking clock banging away next to my ear 24 hours a day, I might have been able to focus much more just on the first element, training people into improved performances. But I was on a mission to turn this business round and sell it within five years and I'd pretty much promised the senior shareholders, most of whom had grown jittery over the previous couple of years, that that's what I'd do.

To this day, I'm still gratified that, during the tempest of those first six months, only a couple of people at Meantime resigned. I think they decided to up sticks because they could see that a very different kind of business was going to be on the way, a business which was as far away from a 'lifestyle' business as I could take it. Lifestyle businesses are unlikely to make money for people other than the owner, which makes them more difficult to scale up; they can face permanent threats of insolvency because of strategic absence, and are unlikely to find a buyer to get them out of trouble because their identity is so deeply rooted in the participants' desire to meld their work with their vision of the life they'd like to lead. Lifestyle businesses aren't a bad thing per se; for those who achieve them and keep them going, they can offer a delightful way of life. (The reality, however, is that most bury huge amounts of stress and strain beneath the gliding surface swan.) It's very unusual, however, for a lifestyle business to attract shareholders; however, if a shareholder does invest, the founder is no longer able to plan his work around his own lifestyle choices. Those few employees who decided it was time to move on did so with good grace and with warm feelings on both sides, partly because I was careful to ask them questions, listen to their feelings, and in doing so I could see them coming to the realisation themselves: this isn't going to be a business I'm going to enjoy working in. They didn't need me to tell them – they effectively told me themselves. In the end I only had to 'let go' one person; everyone else, I'm pleased to say, stayed on board for the ride.

I'd been advised by the board that certain members of the team should potentially be asked to move on, but I preferred to adopt the listening and questioning approach, letting people tell me what they thought needed to happen.

That process enabled me to identify some real gems who, up until that point, had perhaps been in the wrong role. Take Ben Joseph, for example, one of the founder shareholders, a school friend of Hooky's and up until my arrival, effectively the COO.[19] Ben hugely impressed me with his energy, attitude and enthusiasm but I'd come in as CEO and didn't need a deputy. What I did need was someone who loved the business, who had the right attitude and who I could trust to begin to make changes under my direction to the way we operated our entire logistics system. Within months, Ben emerged as an incredibly reliable operations director, becoming a vital member of the team, and to this day remains someone I consider a friend. He acted as a crucial 'glue man' for me, retaining the spirit of the original Meantime and its ethos and enabling the employees to feel that the new era would never get close to throwing the baby out with the bathwater. Ben was always honest, not afraid to tell the truth, or more importantly what you didn't want to hear, while always being one hundred per cent encouraging.

I made some immediate senior appointments. Sales and marketing were going to be absolutely crucial functions in our turnaround, and both were sorely lacking when I arrived. I'd worked with Melanie Smith at SAB Miller in the Peroni years and had always found her motivated, hard working, loyal and reliable. She was my first choice as sales director for Meantime, and I was thrilled when she agreed to join. Another SAB colleague, Rich Myers, had impressed me as a brand manager and I headhunted him to come and join us

---

19 The chief operating officer (COO) normally reports to the chief executive officer (CEO). The former is more concerned with implementation, the latter with both implementation and strategy.

as marketing director; this was a big career step-up for Rich, and he met the challenge with admirable enthusiasm and achieved real success. Both delivered everything I wanted of them and more in the four years that followed; I couldn't have been happier with them. What's also significant is that both came to Meantime, like me, from a very corporate, 'big business' environment and both swiftly adapted to this new way of life in a swashbuckling small business. They both checked in their corporate selves at the Meantime door and adapted to their new lives with amazing vigour and creativity. Just as importantly, they worked well together; in the back of my mind, I'd hoped that by putting a man and a woman together in those two vital positions, we'd avoid some of the unnecessary displays of testosterone you can sometimes get in teams which are predominantly male. I was of course fortunate too in that I'd known them both from SAB Miller days, and the sophisticated SAB human resources information about both their potentials was very clear in my mind.

On the finance front, I botched my first appointment, bringing in a director of finance who failed to live up to my expectations pretty spectacularly: he struggled with the complexity of numbers! Thankfully, I still had Creepy on board as a non-executive director and, true to form, he poked through his address book to find me a replacement quickly. He came up with Bob Emms, who'd previously been at Heineken, and who arrived with us early in 2012. He stayed with us all the way through to the sale, and during the high-intensity weeks and months around the sale proved to be solid as a rock. I had a drink with Bob not long ago, and am pleased to report he remains in excellent form. Also drinking with us that evening was Paul Robinson, who joined Bob in Meantime's finance department around the same time. Paul was part of the audit team working for the accountants we'd brought in to carry out the annual report and he impressed me so much that I offered him a job. Paul is now doing very well at another London craft beer business, Two Tribes, and I'm rooting for him and his new colleagues to pull off something special there.

In 2012, Creepy himself decided it was time for him to move on. In his mind, he'd done the job he'd been asked to do as non-executive director and had brought me in as CEO; he had other priorities in his busy life, which included getting involved in another craft beer venture, Liverpool's Love Lane, whose product I can wholeheartedly recommend; I'm a reliable purchaser of crates of Love Lane to this day and happily report back to him on quality. Once he'd told me he intended to move on, I knew who I wanted to bring in to take his place in the non-executive role: Gary Whitlie, the man who had brought me on at SAB Miller and who had taken my place in Eastern Europe rather than oblige me to move my family out there. Gary knew the beer business better than most, he was wise, he and I had proved our partnership with the Peroni story, and I knew that there could be no better independent advisor to help me through this new challenge. Gary was one hundred per cent great counsel and was reliable all the way through to the sale of the business. Together with Bill, Ian and Tony, I couldn't have wanted a better team of advisors.

Sport analogies are never far from my mind. By mid-2012, as the new manager brought in to turn the club around, I'd managed to sort the finance and get the team into shape with some new star players and a completely different approach to the training ground. We were working now as a really efficient group of colleagues.

Now we needed to start working on results.

Chapter Six

Never Stop Learning

Once I'd moved into the broader corporate area of Bass in 1991 as a sales training manager, I knew I needed to spend the next few years building up my experience. Selling into a working men's club in Dagenham is an entirely different proposition to selling into a national buyer for Sainsbury's. With the former, you don't really have much leeway on price and so you try and increase the odds of a sale by good relationship planning, service and all those key personal skills. When you're selling to a tough national supermarket buyer, they're not remotely interested in those aspects – all they're interested in is price and brand positioning and the cash that generates.

Therefore, in strategic terms, no matter how much work you may do in improving the product or service you are offering, this is of no value in achieving competitive advantage unless it is of value to the user, both your customer and your consumer. The perception of value by the customer might be based on price or it might be based on quality or another metric; the point is, the value that is significant to you, the supplier, is the value that the customer perceives. In this chapter, I'll talk about how I learned to quantify concepts like this by undergoing an MBA,[20] and the thesis I wrote for that set out what I'd learned about customer perception of value from 16 years of selling beer.

The model that I generated for the MBA showed that people will buy, or make buying decisions, generally based on five filters:

- price

- the actual product itself (consumers tend to buy on intrinsics, i.e. 'What does it do?', and extrinsics, 'How does it make me feel?')

- what service they get with it

- the relationship they have with the brand

- how the brand adds value to them.

The more professional the buyer, the more they will lean towards brand and price (which is generally consumer led), while the less sophisticated buyer will be influenced by service and customer relationships. My whole thesis talked about this perception of value and demonstrated that if you don't have the right brand and the right price that is attractive to the consumer, you're never going to get anywhere. So while it's true that people will buy from people they like, it's also

---

20 The MBA is the world's best-known graduate degree in business administration, management and finance. Some young people go straight from university into an MBA programme without work experience; others, like myself, undertake it with a few years' work under their belt.

Never Stop Learning

true that without providing brand or price value, without adding value in those respects, you are limiting your ability as a producer to achieve a sale.

Ultimately, the perception of value is personal and will vary from one person to the next, which is why, as they say, in the land of the blind, 'the one-eyed man is king': anyone who understands the concept of relative value will always have the beginnings of competitive advantage. The best question you can ask a buyer is: what are your *personal* business objectives? Then you can tailor your questions and your presentation to ensure customer and consumer value is at the forefront of your presentation. Most buyers want to know how what you are selling can be monetised.

My first taste of this much bigger world came soon enough: in 1994, I was 'poached' by a senior Bass director, Paul Langley, to work for him as a corporate account manager at Bass Leisure Machine Services (BLMS). Paul, known as 'Chunky', was the spitting image of the snooker star Willie Thorne with his bald head and irrepressible energy. He was so full of ideas that sometimes it was difficult to keep up. This was a vital move for me in several respects. BLMS was the Bass division which looked after the machines which consumers used as a form of relaxation: slot machines, video machines, racing car simulators. With the continued relaxation by the government of the rules surrounding gambling, slot machines were now allowed into betting shops and Bass had its own chain, Coral, which we serviced. But in addition, I began to sell the Bass machines to a wider range of external customers: Ladbrokes, William Hill, Stanley Racing and Tote for slot machines, Granada motorway service stations for the car simulators, national bowling chains like Hollywood Bowl for the video machines. I worked with a fantastic guy called John Loveday who was massively experienced in the machines world, but would always have the generosity of spirit to encourage me to experiment with new machine combinations. He was 55 when I worked with him and had a lifetime's experience but also the generosity of spirit to allow a young man to come up with suggestions. At one point, I proposed to him that we try installing the new basketball consoles in service stations and, although he'd seen these fail elsewhere, he welcomed the trial, and they turned out to be relatively successful. I learned the useful trade knowledge that it was much more difficult to land a ball through the hoop if the ball wasn't fully inflated, so do remember that next time you visit a fairground: always choose the hardest ball!

The job was based back at Burton-on-Trent, so once more I was commuting from home in Newbury, staying in Burton for three or four nights a week, either in hotels or occasionally with my mum in her spare room. I was 29 and travelling all over the country to make pitches to these very senior buyers at national leisure accounts, learning all the time how to develop my sales skills to take on board the much tougher demands a national buyer would make on you. I loved it, and over a two-year stretch, we took a 60 per cent market share of the UK's betting shops – we absolutely nailed it. Two years after I moved on, BLMS was sold out of Bass for £70 million.

There was another reason, though, why I leapt at the chance to take the leisure machine job. It might have seemed odd for a young man with my solid background in beer sales to move out of the brewery business, and in fact there were moves to keep me in brewing by offering me a senior regional beer sales job. But Langley insisted I came to work for him at Leisure and I backed him up all the way because I'd worked something else out too. Some time beforehand (inspired by a top HR director, Chris Edger) Bass had set up the Bass Programme, effectively an in-house senior manager development programme which selected 20 people a year out of a workforce of over 80,000. The programme had been set up in conjunction with management consultancy Deloitte and was hosted by Nottingham Trent University. It pushed those 20 selected individuals first through the Diploma in Management Studies, and then on to a full Master of Business Administration, the MBA. Effectively, Bass had built its own in-house MBA university in order to groom its future potential leaders.

What I'd discovered was that Bass Brewing only ever put forward university graduates for the Bass Programme; if you hadn't been to university, there was no way your senior managers would recommend you. But there was one division in the company which had sent one or two people on to the programme who were not graduates, and that division was BLMS. And once I'd proved to Paul Langley that I was delivering the goods at BLMS as we smashed through our targets, he put my name up for that year's intake of 20 senior managers. I went through a four-day assessment, got the nod and in 1996 embarked on the programme.

This phase of my Bass career was invaluable. By allowing me to study for the diploma and then the MBA, I finally managed to shake that blooming chip off my shoulder. I was attending study weekends in Cambridge, I was spending every Sunday at home locked in my study with piles of academic books to wade through, my young kids doing their best to prise me out. Finally, with maturity and clarity, I was applying myself in a way I'd always known I could, but had as a youngster stupidly refused to. Now I was sitting alongside graduates, making presentations, writing long essays, attending lectures.

There were some great characters on the MBA course. I particularly remember Andy Slee, with whom I spent a lot of time during that period. He and I were endlessly competitive, so much so that we both were given low marks on a negotiation lesson and nearly blew it because neither of us would compromise – a useful lesson in how to lose a battle by being too determined to win. Andy was a big fellow – although incidentally a very good leg spin bowler – and caused endless amusement on one weekend's course when we were all relaxing at a swimming pool; he dived in and created such a huge wave that I was actually thrown out of the pool! He was always on a weight loss programme and one morning insisted on me padding down in my dressing gown to witness his weigh-in, as per the rules of his regime. I couldn't resist secretly pressing a toe down on the scales when he wasn't looking, and he spent the day moaning about how he'd actually put weight on that week. I confessed at the end of the day. Andy and I are firm friends and it was particularly encouraging when he backed me at Meantime by taking a small shareholding himself; that meant a lot to me.

The MBA course enabled me to learn a huge amount of management and business theory and I found it fascinating setting the academic disciplines I was absorbing against my real-life experiences at work over the years. Every one of my jobs, from running a shoe shop to managing pubs and overseeing beer sales at a national level, all of them now made more sense to me within the context of that academic discipline. I was working weekends away with colleagues in Nottingham, sweating over books and presentations and group discussions. I gobbled up the texts on leadership, finance, intra- and entrepreneurship; it was as though I'd been hungry for this context for a long time. There were novelties galore, not the least of which was having to take exams for the first time in 20 years. But also, the course sent me with some colleagues off to South Africa in 2002 to set our learning against an international backdrop, and while out there we were given some on-the-ground glimpses of the realities of life in the townships. Maybe I was fated to join a South African business later on...

The Bass Programme provided me with a roadmap on business and how I might carve out the rest of my career. Overall, I took three years to complete the programme and to pass my MBA. As I had a young family as well as a demanding job, I took three years out halfway through the programme, so finally graduated in September 2002 with my thesis on customer perception of value with regard to beer. It may not sound that exciting to you, but without that intensive period of higher education coming early on in my career, I doubt I would have been picked to run SAB Miller and the Peroni brand in the UK, and therefore I wouldn't have ended up at Meantime in 2011. It just goes to show that you really do reap what you sow.

One of the key books during the MBA was the Johnson, Scholes and Whittington book *Exploring Corporate Strategy* (2007). In my opinion it remains one of the best summaries of strategic thinking in business. The authors make the crucial point that 'strategies develop in organisations on the basis of managers' experience, their sensitivity to changes in their environments and what they learn from operating in their markets.' They summarise the elements of strategic management – analysis, choice and implementation – in this model featured in their book:

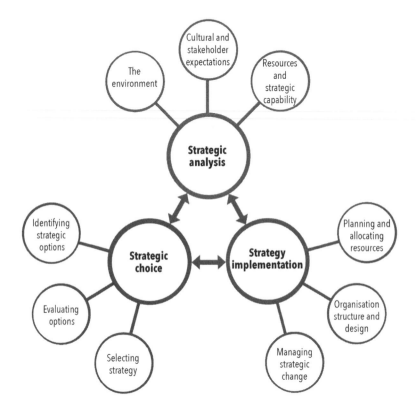

It's a beautifully simple way of representing the interior complexities of business strategy: beginning with analysis, you look at the environment in which you're operating, the situation you face, and the resources you have at your command; you move on to identifying the options available to you, evaluating them and then selecting your strategy; and finally, you implement your chosen strategy and manage that implementation throughout the organisation. That was pretty much exactly how I approached the task at Meantime in 2011. We were taught that business failure roots itself in not conducting the analysis correctly; business is done on gut feel, but if you also analyse, you can validate that gut feel.

I never made a big deal about the MBA and I suspect most of the people I was working with at Meantime neither knew nor cared. For me, though, the fact I'd embarked on higher education once I'd done ten years of work gave my learning a massive edge. For many graduates who go straight from university into an MBA programme, their lack of vocational experience can be a real hindrance: it's too theoretical for them. It's all well and good creating sophisticated models for assessing the role of differing external drivers in consumer buying decisions, but when you've got several years' experience of selling lager into working men's clubs or fruit machines into betting shops, those models are much, much more real. You're analysing behaviour you've observed with your own eyes for a long time. I would always recommend delaying taking an MBA until you've had the chance to let the world knock a bit of sense into you. It gave me the ability to order and filter information.

The MBA also finally confirmed something which my experience had been leading me towards, and which at Meantime became the crucial element in my management approach: you must know your numbers. There's not a single successful business person who can't tell you precisely what the current cash, profit and loss and balance sheet position of their company is. When I got to Meantime, I never ceased to be amazed by some of my new colleagues' lackadaisical approach to numbers. It's not that they didn't care; it's just that they didn't have the experience or the training to know that, without a hold over the numbers, their business was vulnerable. A perfect example was the time when Gary Whitlie, once I'd appointed him to the board as a non-executive director, queried the volumes of beer being produced from each brew. That's what good non-execs do: they ask intelligent and searching questions, but they don't run the company for you. Hooky and I were tasked to report back to the next meeting and once I'd sat down with him, there was a weird anomaly to Hooky's calculations which I couldn't understand. We should have been getting more liquid out of the tanks after the brew than we were getting. I went through every stage with him. Then we spotted what it was: the mash tun was being filled with water without an accurate measure, so each time it was filled, it didn't quite reach the top. The end result of this was that we were producing something like five per cent less beer out of one tank than we could have done. Meantime had been operating at a suboptimal level and in one stroke, just by adding a bit more water, we increased productivity and made a positive shift in the P&L account.

No matter how much you love your product or you love your business, that love has no foundation if you don't know the numbers that make it up.

As is often the case, the arrival of a family – I was 28 when Annie was born in 1993, 31 when Sam arrived three years later, 34 when George completed the family in 1999 – gave me a different perspective on life. Not only was I responsible for these three young people, responsible for providing for them, ensuring they would be able to live in a decent house and go to a good local school; I also wanted to spend the little time my job allowed me to be with them. For me, sport has always been a bonding element in my life and it was no different with the kids: family life as they grew became a whirlwind of lacrosse in the case of Annie, cricket for Sam and skiing for George when he became old enough to show his skills on the slopes.

By my early thirties, I was reaching the point where the combination of intensive work experience across sales, marketing, personnel and finance combined with the intellectual rigour and structure that the MBA course was giving me, could have put me in a good position to move out of the embrace of the Bass corporate world and into a more entrepreneurial role. Success in business depends on lots of things, but I think there are eight core elements, and by the time I was 35, in all honesty, I hadn't mastered all of them; I still had more 'meantime' learning to do before I'd be ready to take on a real entrepreneurial challenge. Here are those core elements:

1. **Energy.** I've mentioned this before: all successful business people are like Duracell bunnies. I've never had a problem with energy, and in my early thirties, I needed that resilience to hold down some big corporate jobs while supporting a growing family. So I'd say I ticked that box pretty early on.

2. **Dealing with complexity.** This is a combination of intelligence and emotional maturity: you can't just know the answer to everything, you need to understand how that answer might work within a given environment of people. This was for me, like it is for many people I believe, a continuous learning curve.

3. **Discipline and focus.** Are you able to 'stick to your knitting', however tempting suggestions to wander off your roadmap might appear? I've been pretty consistent in that area since I decided to do something about my failed A-levels. Can you manage the team so that they stay on message?

4. **Leadership.** Leaders are often born that way but they can also develop. Either way, leadership is a relentless characteristic of enterprise thinking, requiring you to play the role of the Good King effectively and consistently every day. I was getting there by the mid-90s, but I still needed to apply myself to the concept.

5. **Skills and knowledge.** Do you know enough to understand exactly how your business works and what might threaten its success? I'd say, looking back, that I still had much to learn by my early thirties about the bigger world of brand marketing and national selling.

6. **Appetite for risk.** I think this can change over your life. Without a doubt, the arrival of a family significantly dampened mine. Fifteen years later, with the kids now much more developed and semi-independent, things were different. Now? If I'm honest, with the Meantime journey behind me, I'm aware my risk quota has lowered again.

7. **Self-awareness.** Knowing your own strengths and weaknesses and then identifying people who can fill in where you have gaps. I wasn't the finished article in this respect while still at Bass – there were plenty more lessons to come for me.

8. **Luck.** Never underestimate the importance of luck in a successful business career. Somehow, if you fulfil all the other seven factors, the gods will sometimes decide to smile on your feeble efforts and reward you with a stroke of luck. The famous Gary Player quote always comes to mind: the more I practise, the luckier I seem to get.

In many ways, looking back, my thirties were spent filling in the gaps in that list of eight requirements so that when I reached 40 I was headhunted to SAB Miller and began the Peroni adventure. You're not really aware of that at the time, of course; I was just keeping my head down, getting on with life, doing my job as well as I could, being as good a dad as I could be. These are what I mean by 'meantime moments', the phases in your life where you're not obviously learning but, in the background, you always are.

The route to that point, after my stint with Paul Langley at Bass Leisure, was reasonably predictable. I'd made it onto the Bass Programme, which meant that the company expected to get some good return out of me and would therefore move me around to broaden my experience. In 1996, I was moved to national telesales manager, responsible for 300 people manning the phones to capture orders from pubs and clubs for Bass products. (I took over this role from my friend Andy Slee, who had done a tremendous job.) Of those 300, 270 were women and I had a formidable team of six senior managers, all women, with whom I would meet once a week to review performance and set targets. I worked from an office in Burton-on-Trent but the six call centres were spread around the country. These six women terrified me at first, all brightly lit up with fabulous lipstick, looking at me with what I can only describe as disdain. But when I had to make 40 women redundant when we closed one of the call centres in Silvertown in London's East End, back where I'd started my Bass career, I will admit that I shed a tear as I walked around the car park; those women in that office were loyal, supportive, and backed me up in a way that truly humbled me given the circumstances. After breaking the news, I told them all that we were going to go out for an end-of-office night as a group for one last time and they could choose the venue. They chose a medieval-themed restaurant and had me locked up in the stocks all night long.

In 1998, another move, this time to become national account controller managing the Bass accounts with big clients like Tesco, Asda, Sainsbury's. I had 20 account managers for me, working across the board of major retailers, but I was focusing on key clients, particularly Sainsbury's. This is where I really learned the detail about how supermarkets buy, how they use the principle of 'category management' to control the action on their shelves by deliberate placing of products at different points of the customer's journey through the shop. Here, simplistically, is how category management works:

- **staple products** like toilet paper which everyone needs, and which normally don't require much price discounting because people are going to buy them anyway

- **destination products**, like posh bread with seeds in it, which people will seek out once they learn about them

- **seasonal products**, which are relevant to the consumer at only certain times of the year

🍾 **impulse products,** like the sweets deployed menacingly close to the checkout tills (before this was stopped on health grounds).

Beer, on the whole, was and largely remains a seasonal product, bought in bulk by consumers for Bank Holidays, Easter and Christmas, with a few other moments like the World Cup thrown in.

To this day, supermarkets struggle to move beer into a destination product – they just can't compete with the customer experience the on-trade can deliver across the bar, and that key fact was significant when it came to building the Meantime strategy.

So what my job involved, dealing with important clients like Alan Cheeseman at Sainsbury's (their senior beer, wine and spirits buyer), was understanding the drivers guiding Sainsbury's to arrange their stores and their pricing while at the same time protecting and building our brands according to the Bass strategy. Alan himself gave me a really useful lesson one day. An intelligent and scrupulous buyer, he was in that tiny elite club of Masters of Wine, so he really knew his stuff. He came up to Burton and asked me to take him around the local supermarkets: Morrisons, Asda, Tesco and then Sainsbury's. We went into each store and had a good wander around the aisles. At the end of the day, he asked me to summarise what we'd seen. I was at a bit of a loss, so he explained. His own company, Sainsbury's, were in his view missing a trick up here in Burton, by imposing a uniform national product offer onto the Staffordshire region, whereas Morrisons had tailored their offer to promote local favourites like pies more prominently. The further north they went, the more Morrisons managers would put high-carb products like pies near the front; the further south they went, they tended to push green products like lettuce. What Alan had spotted was that Sainsbury's managers weren't appearing to be as flexible in terms of social geography as their competitors at Morrisons. It was a useful lesson in understanding how brand awareness and loyalty can vary according to regional taste.

The world of supermarket buying was a complex minefield, with the additional threat of the government's new consumer pricing regulations: as brand owners, we were not allowed to enter into discussions with supermarkets on suggested price points for our brands. I once came out of a meeting with senior Tesco buyers and one of them pulled me aside:

'Do you realise you broke competition law 28 times in that meeting?'

I'd been way too over-eager, saying things like:

'Well, why not sell that for £4.99 and you could double your transaction?'

I had to learn those rules fast. My boss at the time, Alastair Scott, gave me the wake-up call that I needed. I'd been national account controller for a year and he gave me my annual appraisal in the garden of a pub at the end of Swarkeston Bridge near Donington Park racetrack in Derbyshire. Alastair was a chartered accountant by training but was by no means either dour or constrained by numbers; he was, as I remember, a very good water skier. To this day, I can recall every moment of that appraisal in the pub garden. He told me:

'Miller, you're never going to get where you want to get if

you don't stop being such a bloody salesman. You've got to start taking the enterprise view. If you don't, you've reached as far as you're going to go.'

I was 35 and that was my 'light bulb' moment. Up until then, I'd performed well in every job I'd been in. It simply hadn't occurred to me that there might be a ceiling and I was devastated to discover it. Not everyone is fortunate enough to get a boss with the wisdom and courage that Alastair Scott had to give me the talk I needed to hear, and I'm forever grateful to him for it. It was also him, incidentally, who introduced me to the perceptive concept of 'zappers and sappers': the former are people who will energise you and your business, the latter are those who will drag you down to their lower energy levels. It's a category definition I use to this day. It's as true of your staff and colleagues as it is of customers and suppliers, and overall, your aim should always be to work with zappers and avoid the sappers. A good leader will always try to find and reward people when they do something right, not spend the time criticising them when they do something wrong. Do you try to catch someone out, or catch them before they fall? Alastair Scott, in his wisdom, that day caught me before I fell.

This really was my personal crossroads. I could have elected to settle into the place I found myself in at the turn of the millennium, live a pretty comfortable life and accept that my skills had got me to the point I deserved. I was on a good salary, had a four-bedroomed house and my third child George had just been born. What was to dislike? Well, it wasn't really a matter of disliking anything. It was more a matter of knowing what drove me. Remember, most people I worked with judged me based on my past: cheerful, hard working, full of energy, a good salesman. I'd have that description on my tombstone if I carried on as I was, and nothing wrong with it. Only that's not how I saw myself. I believed I could achieve something much, much more significant, but I never told anyone about it. At the back of my mind all the time was the sense of wanting to make up to my mum for mucking up my education, but wanting also to show my dad, the man I hadn't seen for over 20 years and never would again, that I'd conquered his leaving me and my brother. I can't deny that: I had a massive, hidden internal drive to prove something to somebody who didn't even exist in my life.

Little did I know at the time, but while I was having the harsh realities of life explained to me by Alastair Scott in 1999, another Alastair had convinced some family and friends to put up a little bit of money to start a craft beer business in the back of an industrial estate in Charlton, south-east London. It would take me 12 years before I was to join Hooky at Meantime and, thanks to Alastair Scott, I now had a clear roadmap for my own career development to which I applied myself diligently. I moved on from National Accounts to spend a year developing an in-house Bass internet start-up called Barbox which, while not successful for the group, taught me a lot about the ways in which this newfangled thing called the Web was going to change consumer buying behaviour. We put computers into the free on-trade, including working men's clubs and effectively bypassed our own telesales team. But these were early days for the Internet and while it gave me an insight into the future, it wasn't an immediate success for Bass because we hadn't been able to factor in how to sell up to the retailer in the same way a good telephone salesperson could. That was a really useful lesson: no amount of technology is any good if you have reduced the effectiveness of your sales relationship with your customer. In some ways we were ahead of our time at Barbox and people now are much more ready to be motivated through these technological methods.

During this period, I continued to be fortunate in working for some great bosses. There was John Holland-Kaye, who's now in charge of Heathrow Airport; David Kassler, who founded Phones4U; and David Head, who became Coors' financial director for Europe (now retired). I worked for Kate Doolan for a while, a really impressive operator who had worked her way up through the organisation to become national on-trade sales director of Coors. There was John Holberry, sales director for Coors UK, another director with vision and charisma. These were inspiring people to work for because they all had a natural talent for strategic management and logical forward thinking. They all had that ability to do what I call turning insight into foresight, which is a process of combining your gut instinct with a logical analysis of the competitive environment. I wasn't always the best-behaved corporate manager in these years, sometimes feeling suffocated by the corporate world's processes and politics, but I occasionally managed to let off steam, for example by supergluing all of David Head's office utensils – stapler, pen pot, telephone and so on – to his desk. I'm not sure to this day that he knows it was me! (Sorry, David – I think I caused so much damage he actually had to replace his desk.)

While all this was happening, Bass was reviewing its strategic plans and had sold its brewing facilities, first to Interbrew and then, after that sale had been blocked by the Monopolies and Mergers Commission, to Coors. So overnight, as a Bass Brewers lifer, I found myself part of an American, family-orientated business, guided into a new promotion as director of sales, Coors Brewers UK, by – yet again – Peter Swinburn. Peter made what was to be his last intervention in my career by giving me the opportunity to head up at national level the sale of all Coors beer products into the British on-trade. So, no dealing with supermarkets now, but a big opportunity to develop a national sales strategy to sell Carling, Grolsch, Worthington, Coors Lite, Caffrey's, Tennent's Extra and a few other brands into regional pub chains, brewers and wholesalers.

I spent the next four or five years building my relationships with the traditional British beer establishment: Jonathan Neame at Shepherd Neame, Steve Goodyear at Young's, Paul Baker at Thwaites, Jimmy Arkell at Arkell's, Richard Everard and Stephen Gould of Everards, Scott Waddington at Brains, Denis Robinson of Robinsons, etc.: all the traditional and august members of the Worshipful Company of Brewers, together with some of the newer, up and coming brewers who were part of the Society of Independent Brewers (SIBA), chaired by the remarkable Keith Bott, who went on to receive an MBE for services to the British beer industry. These are inspirational individuals, all of them taking a much longer-term view of their businesses than any public limited company might do because they know they will one day pass the business on to their grandchildren. I remember once ringing up Paul Baker and his secretary said he wasn't in, he was out on business.

'What kind of business?' I asked, cheekily.

'Nick,' she said, patiently. 'Mr Baker's horse is called Business. He rides her every Wednesday.'

I was learning now about my place in the pecking order. I didn't sell much lager to Young's in those five years – Steve Goodyear once taunted me, 'Miller, I wouldn't wash my car with that stuff' – but I built a relationship with Young's which was to be supremely important to me at Peroni and subsequently at Meantime. It's not an exaggeration to say that Young's made both Peroni and Meantime by their commitment to and support of our brand strategy in both cases. They have some supremely talented people like Gillian McLaren, their head of marketing, who was brutally frank in her assessment of our plans but always supportive. I cultivated my relationship with Young's as I did with all of the regional brewers, but Young's will always have a particular place in my grateful memory.

The senior members of the Worshipful Company loved to meet up on shooting parties at country estates around the country, so I had to up my game and learn how to fire a shotgun. It was quite a different world to me, all these fellows from generations of country house living. They were often eccentric, individual and unpredictable, but before long I came to both enjoy their company and respect the deep knowledge they held of the British beer industry. They remain to this day very important in the British beer landscape and parts of their communities: during the Covid pandemic, for example, unlike many landlords around the country, many of the regional brewing families suspended their rent collections from their tenants. These are family brewing businesses which are deeply lodged in their local communities and it's always very sad news to hear of one taking the decision to close. Arkell's, I'm delighted to report, remains in good shape and I still like to think of Jimmy Arkell instructing his pubs in Gloucestershire to put up a hitching post outside every one so that he could ride his horse from one to the other and tie it up while he went in for a pint.

There were innumerable stories from those days. Standing outside in a field one winter's day following a day's shooting, I found myself next to Jonathan Neame of Shepherd Neame.[21] Twenty yards away, Steve Goodyear of Young's was sheltering under a tree which was laden with snow, having a smoke. I nudged Jonathan and winked. He took the hint, loaded his gun and fired it into the tree canopy, dislodging an avalanche of snow upon the unsuspecting Goodyear, who of course subsequently became tagged with the nickname the Polar Bear. They were, and still are, marvellous people whom you underestimate at your peril. One of them, Stephen Gould, managing director of Everards, I went all the way back to schooldays with, as I had played football with him and worked at his future father-in-law's turkey farm, where one of my colleagues was a young girl who would later become his wife. Many years later, I was giving a presentation at the Miller Brands sales conference and mentioned this fact. Stephen was due to come on after me, and his first sentence brought the house down: 'Yes, Nick's right; he and my wife did work together at my father-in-law's turkey farm. She had the good sense to trade up.'

The owners of the regional brewing companies are to this day in very good shape and can teach any ambitious beer executive the facts of business life without raising their heads from the *Racing Post*.

We were, during those years, selling our lager and beer

---

21 Shepherd Neame, with its brewery at the Faversham Brewery in Kent, is Britain's oldest brewer, having started in 1698.

brands into regional brewers like Fuller's, Young's, Everards and Thwaites to sit alongside their products in the offering they were making to their consumers. You might walk into a Greene King pub but fancy a lager, so you could order a Carling or a Grolsch. This is where I began to learn about the complexity of the brewing establishment's relationships, and we began some reciprocal relationships, selling Fuller's or Adnams cask beer back into our network; occasionally, as a Coors man, I'd ask one of those regional brewers to do some brewing for us to top up our own capacity. I might use this as leverage as a means of negotiating with a regional brewer to cooperate with me elsewhere.

During those years I was looking after our route into the market, dealing with the regional brewers, and was ably supported by Paul Jenkins, who dealt with all the wholesalers for us. He was so competent and efficient that I hardly ever needed to get involved in this side of our business, so I was able to concentrate on building my relationships with the regional brewers. Paul was about ten years older than me and he taught me an awful lot: he was one of the best sales managers it's been my privilege to work with. Old fashioned in many ways, he was 'tough as old boots' and I relied on him, showing once again how much you can learn from those working for you as you can from the people you work for, if you're just prepared to listen.

I was learning what Alastair Scott had advised me to do: how to take a holistic, enterprise view of the beer business. At the same time, looking back, I was building my own personal advisory board of supremely experienced beer professionals whose advice I would value for years to come. Yet again, while carrying on in my career, I was 'in the meantime' learning invaluable lessons that would help me enormously during the Meantime years. Yet, not wanting to embarrass myself in front of this new constituency of family brewery owners, I kept my own ambitions to myself. I kept my head down, learned from these unusual but talented individuals, and finally pieced together how the British brewing industry operated as an organic structure whose centuries of tradition were now colliding with a new global beer industry. This was classic enterprise sales thinking which I'd learned over the years: looking at the bigger picture in terms of sales, distribution and consumer taste. It was fascinating, thrilling and inspiring, and after five years of hard graft in charge of the Coors portfolio and engaging with these characters, I knew I had one more task to undertake before I'd be ready to surprise everyone. I knew I needed to prove that I could take all the knowledge I'd acquired up until the age of 40, which I hit at the end of my tenure as director of sales for Coors UK, and take it further by delivering a genuine consumer brand success story. I still had a lot to prove to myself, and the next step was going to be all about engaging with consumers and transforming their notions of a brand.

That brand would be Peroni.

Chapter Seven

The Peroni Adventure

By the early years of the new millennium, the landscape of beer drinking had changed enormously. Whereas at the start of my career, almost 80 per cent of all beer was consumed in a pub, by 2005 only half of it was; the rest was bought in supermarkets, cash and carries and corner shops. When I first worked for Bass, the drinking environment was dominated by the Bix Six brewers; now, the Beer Orders of 1989 had seen those empires dismantled and a wide range of tenanted and managed pubs were controlled by groups like Mitchells & Butlers and Enterprise Inns. Smoking in pubs was a thing of the past, and now you'd be as likely to see a group of mums drinking at a table with a couple of prams beside them as you would blokes standing at the bar. Young people didn't want to drink what their parents drank and they had far more opportunities via the Internet and social media to provide them with greater lifestyle choices.

In the background, the industry was struggling to cope with all these rapid changes alongside increased pressure on existing models: not a year would go by without some newly elected MP (usually without any knowledge of the brewing industry) standing up in Parliament berating a pub group for charging its tenants allegedly exploitative rates for providing them with beer. A pub tenant would sign a contract to take on a pub, and that contract would normally stipulate the price at which he or she would be obliged to buy the beer from the owner. This provided an additional profit element for the group and ensured that the tenant had reliability of service. But unfavourable economic factors or increased local competition could swiftly turn that into a problem for either the owner or the tenant, and so a pendulum swing for the pub groups was developing between favouring tenanted pubs – where the landlord would be left alone but would buy the beer from you – and managed pubs, where the landlord was employed by the pub group. Everyone was chasing margin to manage their cumbersome debt within a social environment where consumers were pressing ahead with their own choices about consumption.

What all this meant was that, for brewers, there was more and more of a need to establish a direct emotional link with the consumer and prove more value to the retailer, processes which needed to be strong enough to override all these differing and often conflicting influences. A link was needed which would work as well in the pub or the club or the hotel as it did in the supermarket, and which would be strong enough to justify the kind of price which would enable the brewer, the pub group and the individual landlord all to make the premium they needed in order both to survive and to grow. My time at Coors, negotiating with all the different pub owners and brewers, had not required me to concentrate on developing a consumer brand; my job during those years was to ship out as much of our existing product as I could through establishing and building relationships with pub owners, commonly known as 'trade marketing'. As is perhaps my habit, I was aware in the back of my mind that I needed to get some solid experience of consumer brand management to add to my career, but I wasn't making any particularly active steps in that direction. I was enjoying my time working with the old English beer families and the wholesalers, and I could have stayed doing that as director of sales of Coors UK for some time. At the same time, I was commuting vast distances, which was tough on family life, and I was aware that I had probably reached the 'glass ceiling' in the Bass/Coors empire. There weren't obvious places for me to go, particularly since my reputation was probably still that of a salesman; the MBA hadn't entirely taken away that image of the in-your-face sales professional as far as the great and the good at Bass were concerned. I was 40 years old and facing a decision: stay put, become a Bass/Coors lifer and enjoy the second half of my career in a relatively comfortable way, or give myself another big challenge.

While I was weighing up these thoughts in a not particularly vigorous way, I got a call out of the blue from a headhunter called John McNeish. He told me that the SAB Miller group wanted to build their presence in the UK, there was a role for a sales director and would I be interested? I was aware of SAB of course: they'd gone from 30th biggest global brewer in 1990 to being in the top five in the space of 15 years. I knew a little about CEO Graham Mackay, how he'd forged this global group by listing SAB on the

London Stock Exchange and then acquiring the American Miller Group brewing business. They were active all over the world, primarily in Eastern Europe and Africa, but in the UK their brands like Castle Lager and Pilsner Urquell were farmed out to distributors First Drinks; other brands they owned, such as Miller Beer, were distributed for them by Scottish & Newcastle; and their niche Italian beer Peroni Nastro Azzurro was controlled by a tightly knit group of seven interlinked Italian wholesalers nationwide.

SAB Miller, in other words, had no direct access to the pub trade or to consumers in the UK, even though the company was listed on the London Stock Exchange, and they'd taken the strategic decision to change that. They wanted to demonstrate to the City that, as well as being a global acquirer of beer companies, they could also develop brands. So Miller Brands UK was going to be the vehicle which demonstrated to the financial world that SAB Miller plc was more than the sum of its parts. The man put in charge of developing this new UK business was Gary Whitlie, who has already appeared in these pages. Gary was the financial controller of SAB Miller, a really huge job, and had worked himself to the bone flying all over the world as the group mushroomed in size. He reported directly to Malcolm Wyman, the overall finance director of SAB Miller and the man who, with Graham Mackay, had built this global empire out of a tiny South African brewery. Now Gary had come back to the UK to build a strategic business here and he'd hired some headhunters to find him a sales director.

The whole process of getting to know SAB Miller, and of them getting to know me, was genuinely fascinating. I'd spent my career within Bass, a very traditional British company which had fairly standard means of assessing its personnel. As I've mentioned earlier, one of my senior jobs came after I'd been interviewed by David Henderson while we were both in bat for the Bass cricket team. Of course Bass had some talented leaders like Peter Swinburn and others, but it never fully embraced the methodology of psychometric testing. SAB Miller tended to make more use of such techniques and it was an interesting contrast. After the initial interview with Gary, I was thrown into a five-hour, one-on-one interview with a psychologist at the headquarters in Mayfair. I was being tested on a range of criteria: how do you deal with complexity? how do you deal with adversity? do you see things conceptually or practically? and so on. As part of the interview/induction process, I discovered that I was classified as ENTP (extraverted, intuitive, thinking, prospecting) on the Myers-Briggs[22] personality indicator. ENTP types are resourceful in solving new problems, often stimulating company and outspoken, but may neglect routine assignments. If you've never undertaken a Myers-Briggs personality test before, then I recommend you do so: it's easily accessible on the web, and I'm pretty sure the analysis you get will prove useful to you in determining what route might be best for you going forward, and where you need to address issues. Better you know those results yourself before being surprised by a future employer. This was the first time in my life I'd been seriously analysed like that and although it was uncomfortable at first, I recognised the value both

---

22 The Myers-Briggs system of categorising people into one of 16 personality types was first developed in the United States in the early 20th century by Katharine Cook Briggs and her daughter Isabel Briggs Myers. It is still today probably the most widely used personality indicator in the workplace.

to me and to the organisation. What's the point, really, in hiring someone if you don't know how they are likely to react to the demands you make on them? During the same assessment period, I was told that I would most likely peak in terms of my professional career at the age of 54; I had 14 years to go.

The one thing I didn't know at the time was that Gary had his eye on me to become a managing director for them, not necessarily in the UK. Being a global group operating in almost 70 countries, they placed huge importance on the selection of country managers, assuming that the elite would be moved around from one country to another to build knowledge and also spread good practice within the group. So while the board at Bass/Coors had been happy to see me trundle along for the next few years as a reliable senior manager, the guys at SAB Miller had spotted potential in me. I'd come up on their radar and they obviously thought I could achieve more than I was currently doing. It's not often that you get that kind of external involvement in your career; it's not often that those senior to you can look beyond what they know of you to what you could actually become. When you get the attention of people like that, you need to respond because the chance may never come again.

A couple of years into my period with SAB I realised the business had plans for me when Gary told me that I'd been nominated to attend the SAB Group Action Learning Programme. Every other year, the company selected 30 senior executives from its operations in 70 countries around the world and threw them together on an intensive training course in the Hilton Hotel in Park Lane, London, for a week. They called it a training course, but in reality this was the process by which SAB selected its future leaders. For that first week, you'd have four or five psychologists taking you through intelligence testing, scenario planning, training modules and observing you closely all the way through. As the UK sales and marketing director, I was also acting as the host for the trade visits which we arranged for that week. I set up a dinner for the entire group at the Lamb in Leadenhall in London, with the team of psychologists sitting at the front. When the food had been eaten, the psychologists asked me to go up on stage and ask the audience for feedback on the trade visits I'd laid on.

One of the 30 executives turned out to be a friend of a colleague I'd crossed swords with since joining SAB, and he obviously decided to take this opportunity to have a go at me. He stood up, told the entire group that the trade visits had been a disaster, that the Peroni he'd been served in the bar I'd sent them to had been warm. He effectively slated me for a good five minutes. I could see the psychologists watching me, wondering how I would respond. While that was happening, two of my salesmen who had helped me set up the trade visits, without any warning and certainly without any instruction from me, left their seats at the back of the room and came to stand behind me on the stage. With them at my back, I decided to respond, told the audience that we were a new SAB business, we had just 25 people in our sales force working to cover 40,000-plus retail outlets in the UK and that I had deliberately not attempted to cherry-pick what I would know to be perfect outlets; we picked them randomly, and hands up, the one the fellow had mentioned wasn't up to standard. So I addressed him directly, thanked him for the feedback, told him that we would improve that outlet but also told him that we weren't going to change the way we operated, and that we weren't in the business of window-dressing for overseas executives. The whole audience stood up and applauded. If I'm honest, I knew at that very moment that I had enhanced my chances of promotion by the way I handled that situation.

At the end of the first week, we were grouped up into smaller teams, and as the UK sales director I was put with Chris Taylor, the SAB global brand director, and Filippo Scandellari, the SAB marketing director for Italy. The three of us were then flown to South Africa to set up a two-week branding exercise there, being monitored all the time, knowing that at the end of it we'd be asked to make a presentation to the executive board of SAB on our findings. On the way back we were dropped into Zambia to advise on a logistics system at one of the SAB Coca-Cola plants there.[23] One of the local team took us to a shipping container in the middle of nowhere which he told us was used to service the township we could see in the distance.

'The delivery fleet will be here in a minute,' he said. A few minutes later, round the corner came one man with a wheelbarrow. This was their distribution network: individuals with wheelbarrows who were incentivised to sell SAB beer and cola into the township by means of an increasing sales commission the more they sold. And it worked: we followed one of the guys on his wheelbarrow trip, watched him make his sales, watched him come back for more and concluded there was nothing we could offer to improve it.

Back in London, we made our presentation to the SAB

---

23 SAB, South African Breweries, was a massive conglomerate, listed on the UK's FTSE 100 and had a significant soft drinks side to its global business.

executive board on what we'd found in South Africa, making constructive recommendations on what we'd improve in the systems. Remember, these board directors had cut their teeth in the South African market so they knew everything about that environment. During our presentation, we also included two slides on the Zambia experience, which basically said: we know this was a wind-up; the system in Zambia is working perfectly well without any need for advice from us three. As a result of that month's programme, all three of us were promoted within six months, along with seven others; four of the 30 were sacked; the other 16 were told they had reached the limit of their careers and wouldn't advance. And the guy who'd stood up to slate me at the initial dinner ended up being demoted a few years later.

Working with SAB Miller was a big step up from the traditional environment of Bass, opening my eyes to a much bigger picture about how beer could be marketed around the world. I was now part of a global enterprise: Cyril Ramaphosa was a non-executive director, Nelson Mandela spoke at the SAB sales conferences. Although the new UK venture was a tiny minnow within the larger global enterprise, there was a lot of interest in what we might be able to achieve. SAB Miller had pioneered global brand architecture programmes, all coming out of its UK headquarters in Woking, and it was impressive in the way in which it communicated to its teams all over the world to impose consistency in brand presentation. It imposed global rules on how senior officials spoke to the press, how purchasing was managed, how personnel were assessed. It was in many ways illuminating, showing me just how much of the life of a business could be measured, managed and quantified.

What SAB Miller hadn't done, though, was build a brand in a Western European market from scratch, and that was the challenge they'd thrown down to Gary Whitlie in the UK. What could we achieve from a standing start? Could we make a real difference in shareholder value for SAB Miller plc right under the noses of the City funds and market analysts?

I still recall to this day the phone call I received from Stephen Goodyear of Young's on my first day at my shiny new desk at the SAB Miller offices in Woking. There was no paper on it; I had a brand new stapler, a pot of new pens. I had a new PA sitting nervously outside, waiting to find out what sort of character she'd been handed, and my phone rang. It was Goodyear, the Polar Bear.

'Ah Miller,' he said. 'How's it going? Shiny desk? No paper on it yet?'

'Yup, that's right Steve.'

'New stapler? Bet it's full of staples, isn't it? New pens? Nice ones, I should think, are they? You got an in-tray? Nothing in it yet, I suppose? Nothing in the out-tray? Marvellous! Now, Miller, tell me what brands you're selling.'

'Stop winding me up, Steve,' I said.

'No, no, I want to know, tell me,' he said.

'Well, Peroni, an Italian-style lager. Polish brands like Tyskie, Pilsner Urquell. We've got Miller Beer. I bet you love American lager, don't you, Steve?'

'Oh very good, very good, Miller! Marvellous stuff. I think I'd like to place an order.'

There was a slight pause.

'Oh, all right,' I said. 'What do you want?' I was actually now quite hopeful that he might genuinely want to become a customer.

'Put me down for one mixed case!' he said, snorting with laughter, and put the phone down.

Before anything else happened that first day, Gary told me I had to spend a couple of hours with PR to draft an announcement about my appointment as sales director.

'OK, where are they? I'll have a quick word,' I said.

'They're over there,' Gary replied, pointing at a group of four people sitting on sofas.

'Gary, there are four of them. Why do you need four people to tell *Brewing Monthly* I've left Bass and joined SAB?'

'It's how we do it, Nick,' he said. 'PR agencies, they never come in packs of less than four.'

So reluctantly, because I've never been a fan of self-promotion, I sat down with them. Their head, a tough American woman, quizzed me and I was quite short in my answers. She wasn't happy with that, and made me go over every detail of my career. Eventually, they drafted a fulsome piece of text which I thought was frankly embarrassing, but they insisted this was what was needed. So to get my own back, I said:

'OK, but you can't release that to the press for five hours.'

'Why not?' asked the tough PR exec.

'I have to clear it with my dad first,' I said, and walked out of the room clutching their draft. America, of course, was five hours behind us.

As I expected, she went straight to Gary, and said:

'Gary, is Nick the son of the head of Miller Beer in America?'

He looked at her.

'Of course not. He's from bloody Burton-on-Trent.'

She told him what I'd said.

Gary just laughed and walked off.

Gary initially wanted me to set up a sales strategy for SAB Miller in the UK, to take ownership of the selling of its brands away from the third-party distributors. We needed to work out a number of things: what was our route to market, what was our pricing strategy, what was our brand and portfolio strategy, what were we going to sell and who were we going to sell it to? What sort of organisation would we need to sell into and service our accounts? What sales tools would we need? What would our customer relationship management (CRM) systems look like? How many people would we need to employ?

I started out that autumn in 2005 with no more than six people working for me, two of whom were Italians I inherited from the current Peroni team, one was fresh out of university, and three young fellows who thought they were hotshot salesmen: one called Scott Russell, who was, and two who were not quite so good. We had no infrastructure, no systems to speak of, no established methods of recording sales and customer information. We had to build everything from scratch. But Gary and I were clear what we were doing there: we were going to change the way that people in the UK thought about beer. Nothing less would do. If we could achieve that, then we would make a real impact on the SAB Miller share price on the London Stock Exchange, and that was a much bigger metric than I'd been working to in my career up to that point. My horizons were suddenly much broader.

We looked closely at the brands within the group and developed a clear strategy for each one, focusing on proposition, pricing and route to market that would be appropriate to the UK. We had Eastern European lagers like Tyskie, we had prestige Czech lagers like Pilsner Urquell, we had a stylish but niche Italian lager called Nastro Azzurro Peroni, and we had some American beers from the tie-up with Miller Group. We also distributed a Czech lager called Kozel, although we didn't own the rights in the UK; a smart Cornish entrepreneur called Rolf Munding had acquired those rights in 1999. By the time I came on the scene, Kozel had become a roaring success in the Czech Republic so our lack of ownership in the UK put us out of sync. I went to meet Rolf to see if we could do a deal. He's an impressive guy, a natural entrepreneur and good company. He asked for a price for the UK rights which I knew was too high. Our contract with him allowed us to inflate the price each year to him, which in turn determined his selling price, so I warned him that if he didn't accept a more realistic price, I was going to put the prices up, which would make it difficult for him to continue selling into his key outlet. No deal, he said. He put up with my pricing tactic for three years, then finally came back to me and said he wanted to sell. I drove down to Penzance to see him with my finance director, Mike Owen. We did a deal with Rolf to buy back the brand at a much more reasonable price, shook hands and then all three of us went for lunch. And then I made a foolish mistake: at the end of lunch, which was a jovial affair with all three of us getting on well, I spoofed Rolf for the cost of lunch and won. (Spoof is a game of chance often played in a pub to establish who buys the next round. Basically it is a guessing game involving coins. Each player draws some number of coins between zero and three from their pocket and holds them concealed within a clenched hand. If more than three are held this is deemed to count as three. The denomination of the coin is irrelevant; it's just the number that counts. The idea is then to take turns to guess the combined total number contained in all the players' hands.)

That meant Rolf ended up paying for lunch, having just agreed to sell Kozel to us for much less than he'd wanted to three years before. On the way back, he rang me on my mobile, serious this time, and said he'd changed his mind about selling and I had to renegotiate on the hoof. For the price of a couple of sandwiches and a pint of beer, I'd irritated him so much that he came back to claw back some more cash on the deal we'd agreed. That was another important lesson: when you're negotiating, always leave the other party with their dignity intact and feeling that they've come out on top. It was a lesson that would really kick in when we came to sell Meantime. Rolf and I, by the way, remained on good terms once I'd got around my dumb error and we've done business several times since.

As we examined the SAB portfolio in the UK, we asked ourselves: what was each brand's consumer proposition, what did it mean to the consumer, and how were we going to position each brand's proposition most effectively? This is where the weighted average market price (WAMP) really came into play: you essentially take the entire UK beer market and you index it on a price per litre versus volume basis. So, as an example, take the average price on this index to be 100, then evaluate all your brands against that average. Carling at that time would have come in as 80 whereas a brand such as Stella might have achieved a maximum of 110. What we wanted to do was to find within the SAB Miller family a brand which could be developed in such a way that it could smash through that WAMP barrier and create a genuinely new premium product in the UK market. In turn, this would create greater margin for us and our customers while fulfilling a consumer need.

During the initial meetings in those first few months in 2005, I concluded that Peroni, the potential hidden jewel in the Miller Brands UK group, could with the right decisions and marketing support come in at 150 on the WAMP scale, blowing away the competition. We were selling no more than 100,000 hectolitres of the imported lager in 2005, but I was convinced that we could turn Peroni from a niche Italian drink enjoyed by occasional diners at smart pizza restaurants in London into a genuine on-trade premium lager. This thinking was all based on market opportunity. The on-trade – the pubs, hotels and clubs – were at the time selling Stella, Kronenbourg and Grolsch. Stella was colloquially known as 'wifebeater' on account of its strong alcohol content, Kronenbourg was French and therefore often inimical to the beliefs of a traditional English drinker, and no one really knew what Grolsch stood for; all three brands, therefore, had weaknesses in their consumer and customer proposition. All three brands were heavily discounted in the off-trade, particularly the supermarkets, which meant that the pubs found it difficult to achieve a price premium because consumers had been taught to expect a lower price. So if the WAMP data set a price of £3.50 for a pint of Carling, it would be pretty much impossible to get more than £4 for a pint of Stella: the brand characteristics wouldn't allow it to go higher. And since people would on the whole drink more volume of Carling than of Stella, because a drinker would 'nurse' a Stella more because of its increased alcohol content and higher price point, then the small price differential between the two would mean that both delivered overall the same kind of profit to the customer.

Our proposition in this respect was very simple: we would recommend £1 more per pint at the bar for Peroni than Stella. And in order to allow consumers to feel that that price differential was justified, we would emphasise through marketing the distinctive elements of the Peroni brand: a cool Italian feel, stylish, individual, making use of unique and expensive-looking glassware, associated with good-looking well-dressed southern Europeans, everything in fact that Stella, Kronenbourg and Grolsch were not. We were trying to encapsulate Italian style into beer. By taking back control of the sales process and simultaneously creating an entirely new brand proposition, we could create a massively successful world beer brand for SAB Miller in the UK market, deliver significant profits and demonstrate to the City that the group was capable of lucratively innovative behaviour. The strategy which we created for Peroni was to inform the entire strategy subsequently at Meantime; I just didn't know that then.

Until our arrival, the pricing of Peroni in the UK was set by the closed shop of Italian distributors based in London, most of whom had clear links back to the old families in Sicily and southern Italy. They were trying to compete with Stella at the same price point, without having the massive backup of scale and distribution and marketing which that brand could rely upon. Stella was brewed in the UK and could be delivered at whatever volume the market required; Peroni was imported from Italy. So the first thing I did was go in to see these wholesalers in London and tell them both that we were going to start distributing directly to customers they already serviced, and also that we were going to increase the price they would have to pay us to wholesale the brand. Inevitably, they were not happy. Muttered imprecations in Italian were made and, just for a while, I felt a little nervous about sticking my size 10 boots into this Italian hornets' nest. But if we were going to win, we had to wrestle back control. It would be impossible to build a premium brand without absolute control over how it was distributed. The salesman I'd inherited when I joined SAB, Scott Russell, turned out to be an invaluable member of the team in handling these negotiations with the distributors.

The brand was known then in the trade as Nastro Azzurro, or Blue Ribbon. Chris Taylor, the SAB global brand director, had already begun to work with a brilliant advertising creative director called Ian Cassie on the development of the brand identify in the UK. We decided to relegate the Blue Ribbon phrase to sub-brand status, and focus on the name Peroni, which was much easier for consumers to remember and to say than 'Nastro Azzurro', particularly when standing at a busy bar. We took all the unnecessary and confusing Italian motifs off the bottle, we put it into a green glass to enable it to stand out from the competition, we did some very stylish design work to match the blue of the brand with the green of the glass, and on top of that we began some top-level PR events.

At the same time, we categorised the outlets we were going to sell to on three criteria:

1. Are their customers our target consumers, the ones that we want to champion Peroni: early thirties urban consumers, well groomed, style conscious, fashion aware? If not, we don't want them as an outlet.

2. Is the outlet's atmosphere and sense of occasion suitable for us? We don't want noise and bustle; we want calm, sophisticated, stylish drinking.

3. Does the outlet look good? Is it smart enough to allow our brand to look desirable? Does it look and feel right?

If an outlet ticked all three boxes, it became a gold outlet; two made it silver, one made it bronze. Whichever level the outlet came into, it still had to have the right consumer; if it didn't sell to our target consumer, it didn't even come onto our list. (In fact, one year, we gave the Miller Brands UK Salesman of the Year award to one of our salesmen who refused to drop the price of Peroni to a well-known chain of pubs which specialised in serving beer cheaply to a not particularly sophisticated customer base – his refusal to let our lager appear in those pubs helped our brand acceleration more than anything else that year.) Once we had assessed our outlets, we created a rewards architecture based on their behaviour: did they train their staff well, did they use the branded glassware we were offering them in the right way, did they use our branded font, would they consider appropriate joint promotions with us? We were relentless in driving home every last detail of the way in which Peroni was presented to and experienced by the consumer, and we measured absolutely everything, recorded it and rewarded team behaviour in implementing our plans.

We picked our sales team very carefully along the same lines. For example, we had the elegant and raffish Manu who sold Peroni for us into the nightclubs and top restaurants of Mayfair. Lovely fellow, who had just that insouciant touch we needed, a bit of his shirt hanging out, tousled hair, confident. I bought him an Italian scooter to finish off his look and he'd whizz around the streets of Mayfair in the evening, looking more like a Peroni customer than a whole team of market researchers could have come up with. Before long, there was word of mouth going round Mayfair about this cool guy who was selling in this really special Italian designer beer, and we found ourselves able to place our brand exactly where we wanted it to be seen.

We supported this whole process with some truly innovative marketing work, and much of the credit for that needs to be given to the brilliant Ian Cassie, who was creative director of an ad agency we employed called The Bank, together with Chris Taylor, the SAB creative director. Ian was – and still is – a charismatic marketing genius. Long grey hair, black clothes, massive Leicester City fan, drove a black Range Rover with blacked-out windows and blasted out Kasabian from his speakers. His career has included managing the band Hot Chocolate and he also suggested to the pop impresario Mickie Most that he should look at signing an as-yet unknown American folk band called The Eagles. (Most didn't take up his suggestion, much to his subsequent regret, I imagine!) The ideas Ian came up with and delivered sealed our strategy of making Peroni the most desirable beer on the market. He reshot scenes from *La Dolce Vita* for a series of iconic cinema ads which we refused to show on TV – we insisted on the exclusivity of allowing consumers to watch these beautiful films in the cinema only because cinema was so much better than TV for allowing a brand owner to target a consumer directly; he created Europe's first pop-up shop[24] in Bond Street in London where the beautifully lit white interior held nothing but a stylish fridge and a white podium holding one bottle of Peroni; he staged a fashion show on one of the bridges over the Thames; he styled the new bottles and all the carefully planned pack promotional material. The only time we failed was when we pursued an ambitious plan to project a hologram of the Peroni bottle onto the interior shop windows of Harrods in Knightsbridge, forgetting of course that when the sun came out, the hologram would completely disappear.

Ian and his team were also responsible for designing the iconic Peroni pint glass: the unforgettable, tall, flower-engraved glass which, in retrospect, seems to encapsulate the brand so well. However – and this is a great example of how we never stop learning – I at first rejected it! Too flowery, I said. Not manly enough. But my team took one look and they all fell in love with it. Their support was unanimous and I bowed to their wisdom. Before long, that glass had become a collector's item, with individual glasses claimed from one bar or another turning up on eBay at ten quid a pop. Not only was the shape, design and feel of the glass delivering an 88 per cent increase in on-sales, it was also boosting off-sales: we discovered that those people who had either bought a glass from eBay or somehow managed to find their way home after an evening in the pub with a Peroni

---

24 A 'pop-up' is a temporary installation erected for a short period, often outdoors, to allow a brand owner to sell direct to consumers in a given environment.

glass in their coat pocket were then prompted to buy Peroni from the supermarket to fill it. It just goes to show: when you hire the right people, sometimes you're best advised to stand back and let them deliver. Ian was so good that when I went to Meantime, I hired him again and he delivered some absolute magic for us there too.

In a similar way, we held firm when it came to the off-trade. We stuck to our premium pricing, had endless rows with customers like Tesco, many of whom had grown used to shipping volumes of Stella at a much lower price, but in time they could see that they could achieve similar levels of profit by selling fewer units of Peroni at a higher price. We still weren't allowed to discuss retail prices with the supermarkets, because of competition law, but by imposing our own resolute high price and supporting that with the brand proposition, we encouraged the supermarkets to fit in with our strategy. Sometimes a supermarket would refuse to pay our prices; usually we were fine with that, because we maintained our brand integrity.

The business model we applied here was very clear:

1. Is there a market opportunity for a brand like Peroni? Yes, we knew because of our analysis of the competitive market that there was an opportunity for high-price, premium lager.

2. Is your brand proposition correct for the opportunity and comprehensible to your consumer and customer? How does it look, how does it feel? Is the brand's personality evident? The work we delivered here with Ian on the brand character was really crucial: Italian style applied to beer.

3. Is your brand positioned correctly in terms of price and availability to your consumer and customer? We spent many hours analysing how we could justify our positioning to our customers and their consumers, the drinkers. Understanding the value chain is key.

4. Is your pricing strategy correct to maximise the market opportunity? We knew that opportunity was at the premium level, so we needed to be clear about the price differential we were going to impose. Once you've reached what you're sure is the correct price, you have to have the confidence to go with it.

5. What is your route to market? Is it secure? Do you have the confidence of your retail partners to deliver your brand proposition? This is all about the human touch, the 'soft' elements of marketing which are so important: your relationships with your business partners.

6. Is your sales team strong enough and sufficiently well trained and motivated to deliver into that market? Are there going to be any 'rocks' in the way that you need to remove to allow your sales team to succeed?

It was a very full-on experience. During the initial two and half years, when I was first sales director and then sales and marketing director, I was commuting into our Woking office from home at Newbury with my head constantly buzzing with ideas and problems. We were building up teams as well as dismantling existing unworkable operations, we were putting in logistics and finance systems on the hoof.

Despite being part of a global group, we were putting things into place as though we were a brand new business. By the time Gary called me into his office in 2008 to tell me I'd been promoted to managing director that memorable Friday afternoon I've mentioned in a previous chapter, when I was aiming to take a 'Poets', we had invested enormous amounts of energy, time and finance to create a business and to promote in particular one brand which could change the face of British beer, and it was working.

Between 2005 and 2011, we were getting an average of 36 per cent growth in sales every year, the fastest beer category growth in the industry during those years. We increased our sales dramatically in just six years: in 2005 we were selling 150,000 hectolitres of Peroni; by 2011 we'd increased that to 900,000 hectolitres, and now the brand sells well over a million. Putting that in a more visual way, and converting it to pints, we were selling just over 26 million pints of Peroni a year in 2005; by 2011, we'd increased that to over 158 million pints. If you lined every one of those pints up in a line, they'd stretch from Land's End to John o' Groats 16 times.

We were selling so much beer that we actually overtraded and ran out of cash because the traditional industry payment terms of 60 days meant that we needed more working capital to actually keep up supplies to our customers. This was in 2009, and I had to ask my finance director Mike Owen to go cap in hand to the SAB Miller treasury people to get a £5 million loan to see us through. That experience alone was really important for me by the time I came to Meantime because I knew that we would be on our own and wouldn't have a big PLC treasury account to borrow from – I was always worried, as we began the explosive growth in sales at Meantime, about overtrading.[25] I was always checking on our cash reserves. Going from Peroni to Meantime, I would argue that between 2011 and 2015, Meantime achieved the fastest beer category growth in the industry too. The reason both did was the clear focus on fulfilling all the requirements for the delivery of a higher-priced premium beer offer through the retail trade to the consumer.

We had some great people working with us at the time. Finance director Mike Owen was consistently strong, and our supply chain director Martin Harlow was brilliant and subsequently came to do some consultancy for me at Meantime. Martin had the incredibly difficult task of matching deliveries of Peroni from Italy with the rapidly accelerating demand we were creating and at one point came up with the classic comment:

'Nick, we're going to need a bigger boat.'

There were other great characters like Ed McKenna, who I recruited from ABI[26] to help build our sales operation in Ireland. I'd actually had Ed in mind for some time after a great incident on a cricket field a year or so before. It was always a tradition in the brewing industry cricket scene, which was both convivial and highly competitive, for a team to try and sneak in a top professional player to give an edge. A year before I joined SAB, I'd put together a Bass cricket team to take on Thwaites and managed to persuade two semi-pro West Indian fast bowlers to come and play on my team. As we were all

---

25 'Overtrading' occurs when the amount of sales orders creates an issue with the working cash in the business because the sales incomes don't arrive in time to pay for the raw materials and so on required to service them.
26 Anheuser-Busch InBev is the world's largest brewer, based in Leuven, Belgium. It has approximately 630 beer brands in 150 countries.

changing before the game, the Thwaites boys called out:

'Oy Nick, who are your two new team members?'

'Oh, they're with us on a work experience secondment,' I said.

On the pitch, these two brilliant fast bowlers were delivering at speeds of up to 90 mph. Ed McKenna came in to bat for Thwaites – he was a good cricketer and even though he worked for ABI, Thwaites had managed to persuade him to join them that day. I was trying to slate him on the pitch as much as I could, telling my two-star West Indian fast bowlers that this fellow sold 'wifebeater' – ABI's star brand of course was Stella. But no matter how fast and well they bowled, and no matter how many pathetic jibes I made, Ed stayed in place and scored 97 not out. It a was truly impressive example of grit and talent, and once I'd joined SAB I sought him out to join us. Maybe the Henderson recruiting method of conducting an interview at the crease had influenced me, but Ed also passed all the tough psychometric tests as well.

Ed was closely involved with me in the delicate negotiations we had to undertake on behalf of SAB in Ireland. Heineken had bought Amstel in South Africa, removing the competitive advantage in that brand that SAB had built up for years, and this gave us the rights to end the agreement on Miller Beer being sold by Heineken in Ireland. So when I became MD at Miller Brands, one of the first things I was told was to go to Ireland and work out what we were going to do: were we going to stay with Heineken or should we move to another distributor? Top of the list of potential distributors was a successful Irish businessman called Barry Connolly. When I balanced the two up, it was pretty clear that by staying with Heineken, we'd make twice as much profit than if we moved to work with Barry. But it was made clear to me by up-on-high in SAB that, because of the South African situation, they wanted me to choose Barry against Heineken for Ireland.

All this took place over a busy Christmas. Together with our brilliant in-house lawyer Adrian de Souza, Ed and I went into negotiations with Barry and I couldn't work out how well informed he seemed every meeting we had. What I didn't know was that Barry had got one of his own employees to be the cab driver, so after every meeting, when Ed and I would head off back to our hotel or to the airport in a cab and would discuss the meeting, Barry's employee would be up front wearing a cap and making detailed mental notes! He was and is a star operator, Barry, endlessly inventive in his tactics: at one point, while Ed and I were in a meeting with Heineken, a messenger entered the room and handed me an envelope. Inside it, in Barry's handwriting, were the words 'I know what you're doing' together with a smiley face.

The six years I spent at SAB Miller obviously prepared me for the adventure at Meantime, but I also left feeling that I'd delivered. When I joined as sales director in 2005, there were less than ten of us in the business; when I left in 2011, there were 180. In the first three years of our trading, we lost £18 million as we invested in Peroni; when I left in 2011, we were making £40 million every year. The Peroni story probably added one pound to the SAB Miller London Stock Market share price, equivalent to around £1 billion in value. I pointed this out to Graham Mackay at one point, and cheekily asked him if that increase in value was going to be reflected in my bonus. He just looked glassily at me and changed the subject. I understood his position: I'd signed up to a generous salary package and I'd delivered, end of story. But from my perspective, that was another signal: out there, outside of the corporate, salaried world, might it not be possible to deliver this kind of business performance and get properly rewarded for it?

Over that period, I got to know Graham Mackay pretty well. I think he enjoyed my enthusiasm and as a South African with limited knowledge of the UK's beer market, he would gently interrogate me about it. Always a twinkle in his eye, he was a truly impressive man: very cultured, with a love of classical music and opera, he also had a deep belief in the importance of social responsibility in business, believing passionately that business and society were inextricably intertwined. That belief led him to forge SAB's remarkable programme of social and healthcare work throughout the African continent. He was a brilliant listener but occasionally even he was sometimes fazed by English eccentricity. Once, I took him with me on one of the brewers' shoots because I thought it would be a good opportunity for him to meet the established British brewery owners. At one point, Jimmy Arkell of Arkell's beer came up:

'Graham,' he said, with a big grin on his face. 'I've come up with a brilliant idea for Arkell's. I'm going to brew a new lager called Pilsner Arkell, and you'll get so cross with me for imitating Pilsner Urquell that you'll sue me for copyright infringement and I'll get more press coverage than you can buy hot dinners! Go on: sue me!'

Graham looked at him uncomprehendingly, shook his head and walked on. Jim was creased up with laughter.

Graham used to get me to tag with him when it came to announcing the SAB Miller plc annual results to the press in the UK. Every year, we would sit down with the PR team and agree who was going to talk to whom. Inevitably, I'd be told I was going to talk to the 'red tops' – the *Sun*, the *Mirror*, and so on – while Graham would brief the broadsheets like the *Daily Telegraph* and *Financial Times*. One year I said:

'Tell you what Graham: why don't you let me brief the broadsheets this year?'

He looked at me in that way he had.

'Just stick to what you're good at, Nick,' he said. Yet I also knew that Graham wasn't averse to needling my old boss at Coors, Peter Swinburn, telling Peter that Coors had lost out by letting me leave for SAB, and he relished telling Peter just how many hectolitres of Peroni we were selling.

Looking back, those six years at SAB Miller were also about building a team that could make such an incredible difference to the UK beer market. Going from ten people to 180, we built the business based on the clear set of five global SAB values, which I can remember to this day, and which were driven into everyone who worked with us:

1. People are our enduring advantage.

2. Accountability is clear and personal.

3. We work in winning teams.

4. Our customers and our consumers are our focus.

5. Our reputation is indivisible.

Perhaps that list in itself sounds quite 'corporate' but I have come to conclude that a company and the brands it sells must have a clear set of values governing its overall strategy and its day-to-day working practices.

We were part of a big corporate group but I always insisted that my people felt like they were part of something special, something unique. I remember the corporate HQ in London issuing a new edict that SAB Miller plc would incorporate dress-down Friday to encourage team bonding. So I responded by telling all our people in Miller Brands UK that we'd dress casually from Monday to Thursday but we'd all dress up smart on Friday. I wanted us to feel different, special, bonded to each other. We were a young team, vibrant, focused, energetic, creative; we were a million miles away from the steady, easygoing traditional behaviour of Bass and I wasn't going to let anyone feel that tomorrow might be just another day.

As part of that desire to give our team at Miller Brands a sense of individuality within the broader SAB group, I refused to do standard sales conferences at a dull location in the UK; instead, I took the entire team on a company conference to Enschede, the home of Grolsch – all 150 of them. Part of the reason was that half the team hadn't even visited a brewery before because SAB had no breweries of its own in the UK. So it was a chance to get to know the brewers at Grolsch, a process which included a big party in the brewery where all of us, including the Grolsch brewery band led by the MD, Rob Snel, did the Village People YMCA dance and all 150 of us Miller Brands people did a massive conga around the maturation tanks. I got a bollocking from on high for that trip, so the next year I repeated it by taking the entire organisation to Ireland for a memorable conference which included the Kozel brand manager bringing a live goat onto the stage for her presentation – the animal featured on the Czech lager's brand label. Inevitably, the goat emptied its bowels all over the presentation stage, causing much hilarity.

On the plane over to Ireland, I sat next to a young lad called Patrick Mooney, who worked in our logistics department for Martin Harlow. Patrick was a quiet lad and we were trying to bring the confidence out in him despite his inherent shyness. On the plane, he was looking nervous and I asked him what was wrong. He told me that he'd been told to give a speech about our logistics at the conference. I told him that the best advice I'd ever had about speech nerves was to look out at the audience and imagine they're all sitting on the toilet. And lo and behold, a couple of days later he walked up to the podium in front of almost 200 people, grinned down at me in the front row and mimed pulling a toilet chain before going on to give a cracking speech.

Four weeks later, back in the HQ in Woking, I walked into the office late on a Friday and said to our finance director, Mike Owen:

'I don't know what it is Mike, but there's something wrong here.'

Mike said that he had that feeling too. It's part of that whole leadership question, having a gut feel for the health of your business. We left for the weekend, came back in on Monday and, again, there was this sense that things weren't right. I was in a meeting with my big European boss when I saw our head of HR standing in the doorway, crying. I went out and heard the news: Patrick had suffered an epileptic seizure at Clapham Junction station on Friday afternoon and had fallen onto the tracks and been run over by a train. I had to go upstairs and tell the entire Miller Brands team that we'd lost one of our own. SAB Miller behaved impeccably and looked after Patrick's family well beyond their legal requirement. For us, it was a terrifically sad moment but one which, oddly, brought us all even closer together, as adversity can sometimes do.

Throughout this period, I was blessed with a fantastic team around me. I had a brilliant sales director in Darren Tendler, a natural leader and an off-trade specialist. He was succeeded by another great guy, Leo Murphy, an American with buckets of positivity – you always knew from the call of 'Hey man!' that Leo was in the office. Julia Wellard was our HR director, a truly empathetic person but tough when she needed to be. Liz Slater was our supply chain director, calmly efficient and impressively organised, and Sue Clark, who reappears during the Meantime story, was our non-executive director. Ed McKenna delivered for us particularly in Ireland. John Littleton was our corporate affairs and project development manager. All these people were top-drawer, class acts. And we weren't a 'laddish' beer company: our board had an excellent gender balance and we had 25 different nationalities working for us by the end. The fact that we were such a cosmopolitan group really helped us to drive the unique experience of Peroni in the market.

There were so many learning experiences for me to take on into the challenge of Meantime. There were so many similarities: although Meantime was a minnow and SAB Miller was a giant, the actual UK organisation I ended up running, Miller Brands UK, was effectively a start-up in 2005. We spent the first two years building a business, creating departments, functions, roles. By the time Gary came to hand over the reins to me by making me managing director in 2008, we'd built a structure that could cope not just with building a massive brand like Peroni, but also could service and grow all the other brands in our portfolio like Tyskie and Lech lagers, Pilsner Urquell and Miller Genuine Draft.

The decision to charge £1 per pint more for Peroni turns out, in retrospect, to have been a billion-pound decision, and you don't get to make many of those in your career. Let me explain. You're charging £1 more per pint; there are 176 pints in a hectolitre. From 2005 to today, there's been about 10 million hectolitres of Peroni sold. Ten million times 176 is £1.7 billion worth of increased value into the market, which is shared between the retailer and the brand supplier, i.e. Miller Brands UK. Not a bad result, which as I said was probably also mirrored in a similar increase in value through the rise in the SAB Miller plc share price.

By 2010 the whole machine was operating brilliantly but I was nervous about the future. What if Peroni's growth were to plateau? What if a competitor who'd been watching what we were doing decided to have a go with a similar tactic? That's when I decided to begin investigating Plan B and called in all those consultants to help me identify that a little-known craft brewer in Greenwich called Meantime could be the next big thing for SAB Miller. Thankfully for me, my boss at the time slapped me on the wrists and refused to sanction the proposal to acquire Meantime. His attitude and my frustration with not being able to act on what was clearly the correct market analysis would lead me to accept Creepy Crawley's invitation to jump ship and head down to Greenwich.

I'd delivered for Graham Mackay and the SAB Miller board and I'd enjoyed every second of it. But if I couldn't make decisions for myself that I knew were right, then it was time finally to step away from the corporate world. I wanted to test whether I'd learned enough over the last 25 years, while in the meantime working for corporate bosses, to give me an opportunity finally to have a genuine personal success of my own.

I agonised over the decision before eventually taking the plunge.

Chapter Eight

In the Meantime

It's clear to me that while we're going about our lives, doing the things that we do, enjoying our pleasures and earning our livings, there's something else going on in the background. It's almost like those parallel universes that they talk about in quantum physics, when two or more entirely different things can be happening at the same moment. Even before I stumbled upon the Greenwich brewery, I'd categorised this in my mind by the phrase 'in the meantime': you may think you're learning how to be a good salesman, but in the meantime you're learning an awful lot about human psychology. You accept a promotion into another part of the company in order to get more money to buy a bigger house, and in the meantime you're expanding your knowledge about a subject which will be really useful to you in ten years' time. Building your memory banks is crucial to your career: it's the 'shoe leather' of life.

We all work like this. Like it or not, we absorb experience and learning and we store it somewhere; the trick is to keep an eye on that store cupboard as your career develops and check that your ingredients are spread evenly. I was able to take up Creepy's challenge to move to Meantime because I knew that I was ready. I'd had enough relevant experience to be confident as I went in that within five years we'd be able to turn a failing brewery into a company that could be sold for at least £50 million. If I hadn't tramped those streets in East London knocking on the doors of curry houses trying to sell them Carling; if I'd not had the opportunity to get to know the key figures in the traditional British brewing community and build up relationships with them; if I hadn't been plunged into thrills and spills of brand-building at Peroni, then I simply wouldn't have known how to set about rescuing this ailing business. There are a few individuals who have succeeded without 'putting in the time' and I take my hat off to them, but they are rare.

Most people who succeed in business do so because of this process. A small minority of highly unusual and talented men and women are able somehow to bypass this and achieve entrepreneurial success without putting in the time; most business people achieve success after their 40th birthday because they've had the time to pick up the skills they need to win. So if you are young and ambitious then I urge you always to be inquisitive and to treasure those 'meantime moments', and when you're knackered at the end of a tough week doing something to earn your pay which hasn't filled you with the joys of spring, then just sit back and remember that at some point in the future, the lessons you've learned are going to help you do something very special.

That was my reason to give up on the corporate life in 2011: I was ready and, quite literally, I was in the Meantime.

Meanwhile, the market was ready for a new premium offer at the bar. For six years, pubs such as the Young's chain had benefited hugely from the impact of Peroni stepping up as a premium lager. But consumers can be fickle and in the contemporary world want their palates refreshing. The time was right for another premium offer in bars and pubs, and this time it couldn't be another international lager. It was time for a craft beer, particularly an ale.

It was vital for me to prove I was right about the assessment I'd made about Meantime's potential while still at SAB Miller. I wanted to put into practice everything I'd learned along the way during my career and in doing so make this wonderful little craft beer company the success it deserved to be. I had the desire to do that for selfish reasons; there's no shame in admitting that: I didn't spend weeks negotiating with Creepy and the board over my contract and my bonus and share package just for fun – I knew I could turn success into a financial benefit for me and my family. But I'm a team player, always have been, and I wanted to do this as part of a team who would all benefit alongside me. I need to be part of a team because I know I'm not good enough at every part of the business to do it on my own. There's just no kind of business area I could or would have gone into which would result in me being a sole beneficiary, and to that extent I feel more comfortable with the idea of intrapreneurship rather than entrepreneurship. Now, seven years on from the Meantime sale, I'm still able and very happy to meet up with ex-colleagues from those intense times, share a beer and a laugh with them, in the knowledge that they benefited from the sale of the company just like I did. We made it happen together.

Some of the early problems I've already touched upon – the potential failure of the EIS fundraise, the damaging contracts with BrewDog and Adnams – may have been more worrying for me than for some of my colleagues because I was really the only one in the team who had a clear roadmap in my head about what needed to happen over the coming five years. Even so, we dealt with those problems as a team, and everyone, from Hooky himself down to the hard-working men and women on the brewery floor, committed themselves to the task with incredible vigour, loyalty and integrity.

In some senses, all of us at Meantime in 2011 knew what was needed: we had to define what was so special about the beer and the brand which Hooky had created 12 years before, we had to clear the path to enable us to get that message out to the world, and we had to deliver the beer to our customers consistently, passionately and authentically. We'll come to the second and third elements in due course, but it's important initially to focus on that first one. What *was* so special about Meantime beer? And how had Hooky managed to create it?

Well, to answer that we've got to look at how the trends in beer had evolved over the previous decades. Up until the 1960s, the British drank cask ale served in dimpled glasses and warm at around 9° C. Then towards the end of that decade, keg beers and lagers were introduced, around the same time that the British began to enjoy things like package holidays to the hot beaches of southern Spain, where a chilled lager under a beach umbrella felt like magic. Consumers discovered that they actually liked their beer served cold, closer to 4° C than 9° C, and they actively sought out the keg beers at the bar which would satisfy their thirst in the way that a chillier beer would in comparison to a warm ale. Real ale made a bit of a comeback here and there, but keg beer was here to stay. By the turn of the millennium, it was no longer a question of whether a beer should be chilled or not; that was expected. But what the new generation began to demand, as I've described earlier, was more flavour, more storytelling, more localisation, more sustainability, more character-signalling: look at me, I'm a craft beer aficionado.

Hooky, as a natural gourmet, was open to those ideas. In addition, his deep interest in brewing had taken him to Germany at an early age, which was historically the home of that European method of beer brewing which produced the clean, cold and often flavoursome taste of lager and tanked beer. (The soft water of Germany is better suited to lager; Britain's primarily hard water leans more to ales and porters.) The great breweries of Germany and the nearby Czech Republic had for centuries mastered the art of wort distilling and yeast fermentation to produce the highly prized Pilsners for which they were rightly famous. What was distinctive and intuitive about Hooky was that he put two and two together: he understood the changing tastes of London drinkers and he knew more authentically than most British brewers how the Continentals had perfected their trade and continue to do so.

For 12 years, Hooky and his team had produced some truly great beer. At various points, the industry recognised that, particularly when he struck a deal with Sainsbury's in 2007 for Meantime to supply all the beer for their Taste The Difference range. All those punters standing at the bar at The Union in Greenwich would have told you the same thing: this stuff's bloody lovely. So why, by 2011, was the business staggering, reduced to contract brewing for a combative Scottish competitor and scarcely visible as a brand to a whole new generation of consumers who would be primed and ready to adopt the brand? Because the passion and skill and intelligence which Hooky had distilled into Meantime beer hadn't been encapsulated as a brand in anything remotely like an industry-professional way. It was a brilliant craft beer managed by craftsmen, which was why hardly anyone knew about it.

So that's why the first thing I insisted on when I arrived was that we cease production of cask ale. About six per cent of Meantime's turnover came from the cask ale it licensed Adnams to brew for it, and for a business struggling to break even, it was a fairly risky decision to jettison even six per cent of our cash. But strategically, it was obvious: Meantime was a craft beer; it was associated with all the consumer desires and brand characteristics which placed it a million miles away from the land of real ale and casks, so what on earth were we doing introducing doubt into our consumer proposition? What were we saying: Meantime is a craft beer company but we like a bit of real ale too? Absolutely not. The loyal customer doesn't want to hear doubt from his or her favourite brand, so the casks were out.

Having cut out the Adnams cask ale and committed to ending the BrewDog work (these two contracts accounted for almost a third of the beer making up Meantime's output in 2011), that reduced Meantime's output of actual Meantime craft beer when I took over from around 15,000 hectolitres to around 10,000 hectolitres. There, very simply, was our immediate brand problem: we weren't making and selling enough beer to be recognised by consumers as 'a brand'.

We were a niche craft beer, known to and loved by a small number of devoted followers. To put this into context, by the time we came to sell the business four years later, we were selling ten times that amount of beer, almost 100,000 hectolitres of beer, 17.6 million pints. That, by anyone's standards, is a phenomenal rate of growth.

On top of brand focus and volume, there was the issue of price. My analysis the previous year at SAB Miller had demonstrated clearly that there was room in the market for a premium ale to hit the kind of WAMP figures (see Chapters Two and Seven) of 140–150 which Peroni had managed to achieve as a premium lager. In other words, we would explain more clearly to the consumer what the brand was all about; we would sell more of our beer so that more consumers would know us and love us; and we would charge more for every pint because that would bring us more revenue while also rewarding the retailers who bought into our strategy. This strategy was encapsulated into one sentence:

> Meantime will pioneer and change the way consumers think about beer by brewing and selling high-quality premium craft beers.

In order to achieve our objective, we would have to operate as a coherent team at a very high and committed level. I'd learned this at many stages in my career, but most recently at Miller Brands UK when we had driven the growth of Peroni by instilling an absolute commitment within our small part of the global SAB Miller group. We had operated like an ambitious small business; now, at Meantime, we actually *were* an ambitious small business, so I needed everyone, from directors and shareholders through to brewery workers, to sign up to how we were going to behave. I gave us a set of operating principles right from the start:

1. We are a brand-led company and we will never compromise on the quality and premium nature of our beers.

2. We are passionate about our craftsmanship and will celebrate the provenance, styles and quality of the beer.

3. We are entrepreneurial and innovative and we are prepared to challenge and change the UK beer environment.

4. We produce consumer-relevant products that will add value to our customers' offer.

5. Our people have clear responsibilities and account-abilities and they will be measured on delivery.

6. We celebrate and reward success.

7. We work and win as a team. Our decision-making process considers the company first, the team second and the individual third. We will not tolerate internal politics or personal agendas.

8. The strategy is absolutely sacrosanct and will not change unless approved by the board.

9. We have fun.

The other analogy which often strikes me when I come to talk about the Meantime experience is that of the orchestra. No one doubts that the cellists and the viola players and the bassoonist at the London Symphony Orchestra are able to play at the top of their game, but why then do they need this fellow standing in front of them holding a baton? They need him to keep the orchestra in time, working together and maintaining absolute commitment to the score from the very first note to the last. This is really what leadership means: recognising and confirming the skills of your team and then putting in place the methods and practices which will allow every team member to put in his or her best performance every day that they come to work.

Like the conductor, the effective leader needs to be able to pick up on hints, gestures, feelings; you need to have an instinct for how your team are feeling. Are people happy, or is there a sense of underlying concern? Is there a pocket of resistance somewhere, or is everyone working together? These are quite nebulous concepts but they come back to the importance of listening over stating. And proximity to the people you're working with is absolutely vital: being close to people on the shop floor. The leadership at Young's is a brilliant example of this: the likes of Stephen Goodyear and Patrick Dardis know what's going on at head office in Young's because they work there, but they also know every single pub in their estate and most of the staff who work in them by name. Both Stephen and Patrick are so close to their business that they can 'smell it'; they know the temperature of the human resources environment because they get out there and check it. You can reference countless other superb leaders like Julian Richer at hi-fi retailer Richer Sounds or James Timpson at Timpsons locksmiths and shoe repairs, and they all share that same ability to stay close to their staff even as their business mushrooms in size. No matter how successful a senior executive gets, when he or she moves from managing an area to managing a larger territory, then a country, then an international region, the truly successful leaders retain the ability to 'land', to situate themselves whenever they need to among the people actually delivering the service on the ground floor.

Businesses don't succeed when there is a culture of laziness or of self-aggrandisement or politicking and, in truth, people don't really enjoy working in organisations like that. People on the whole want to win, they want a purpose, and your job as leader is to enable them to do that. As a leader, you're aiming to spot them when they do something right and to recognise them for it, to reward them. I learned a long time ago, mainly during my time in the East End of London working for Bass, how to pick up on an atmosphere: I'd walk into a pub and I could tell almost immediately if something was going to 'kick off', and my instinct was normally right. My job now at Meantime was to learn really fast how our various teams and all our individual staff felt about their jobs, their careers and the strategy I was setting out for them. And there wasn't the luxury of time to make any mistakes.

By Christmas 2011, everyone at Meantime was on board for the challenge. One or two Meantime originals had stepped away, including Peter Hayden, who had been a great supporter of Hooky in previous fundraises, investing his life savings, and had brought in his own contacts to support the business. Peter had done a good job as marketing director before I'd arrived, but he felt that it was time for him to move on as he had the opportunity to run his own brewery. I was very pleased to be able to give him the good news about his shareholding four years later. Through the regular town hall meetings, the conversations at the bar of The Union on Friday night, the frequent one-to-ones, we all knew what we were going to do: we were going to make Meantime the biggest success story in British craft beer. Once we had dealt with the problems surrounding the EIS raise by spring 2012, I knew we had the new capital to be able to invest in the key things we needed to do to begin growing. The obvious focus, in those early days, was brewing capacity: if we were going to grow as rapidly as I predicted, we were going to need more tanks and more space.

When I arrived in 2011, Meantime was occupying the back two units, Units Four and Five, of a five-unit warehouse on Blackwall Lane in Greenwich. The other three units were taken up by a tile shop on the main road in Unit One, and then Units Two and Three between the tile shop and the Meantime brewery were occupied by the National Maritime Museum as a storage facility. Being both nosy and also wishing to be a good neighbour, I got to know the museum people well early on, and they'd let me wander around looking at priceless gems like the uniform Nelson wore at the Battle of Cairo. It was like something out of that film, *A Night at the Museum*, and I loved it. Their need for security was understandably so great that every so often reputedly someone would see an SAS soldier flitting over the roof in full gear, trying to test the locking mechanisms. (In case you're thinking of having a go yourself, the museum have since moved their storage facility!)

Unit Four was our warehouse in 2011 while Unit Five was where all the brewing was done. Hooky had set up a basic visitor centre in a room within Unit Five which was pretty unprepossessing and not very welcoming, and we also had a very scruffy little sales office next door. We had to make more space if we were going to make more beer, it was as simple as that. So with a slight sense of trepidation I moved the entire non-brewing staff – admin, sales and so on – out of the Blackwall Lane units and into a purpose-built office half a mile away in the centre of Greenwich in Norman Road. My trepidation was mainly about the potential impact of splitting the team into two, but needs must: we had to have more space to brew and to entertain visitors on guided tours. This move enabled us to open up a much smarter visitor centre with a separate sampling room and, before long, we were entertaining over 300 different visitors a week under the incomparable guidance of Big Al, chief guide, taster and general maverick. I needed people to be able to experience the brand close up, taste the beer coming out of the tanks, go home and tell their family and friends about it, generally spread the word.

Next on the list was logistics. We had too much space taken up with the chaos surrounding our own uneven truck distribution process, so working closely with Ben, we outsourced all our distribution to DHL and in one go cleared up a lot of clutter in Unit Four. Rather than trying to deliver everything in bits and bobs ourselves, we were now using more industry-standard pallets, which were far more efficient, and we also took over a warehouse in Woolwich to store materials and stock. Now we had more space in Unit Four and also in the outside yard because we'd shifted personnel and materials, so we could then spend some of our new investment round on new maturation and fermentation tanks.

We would still need plenty more space though if we were to achieve the levels of brewing in our business plan.

Thankfully, my smoking habit came in handy here. On my regular fag break outside the brewery, I'd got to know Barry, a top man (he joined us later and worked for Ben), who was in charge of the Unit One tile company's distribution and he hinted to me that he thought the company was going bust. I'd made sure I'd already got to know the overall landlords of the whole five units, so I put in a quiet word and within a few months, the tile company did indeed go bust and we took possession of Unit One in 2013, all the while carefully maintaining diplomatic relations with the Maritime Museum – it was important that we always acted as good neighbours. They were probably nervous enough already about the nation's maritime treasures being stored cheek by jowl with a bunch of beer drinkers! But they were solid people and even allowed me to run a pipe from one of our tanks in Unit Five all along the wall of their two storage units to let beer into a new tank we installed in our new space in Unit One. Then we added a brand new kegging line into that front unit, added a small five-hectolitre testing brewery and began to build the new visitor centre.

Use of space, then, over the four years from 2011 to the sale in 2015, was of utmost importance. It was one of those plates it was my job to keep spinning, alongside all the other plates: the daily concern about cash levels, the need to build brand awareness swiftly, the requirement for more and more salespeople to create demand. Space though was always crucial and we were forever trying to work out how to squeeze more capacity into a limited space. In due course, by the end of 2014, we had enough space to bring all our non-brewing personnel back from Greenwich town centre into the Blackwall Lane plant into a swish new first-floor office space and we converted the bulk of the road-facing Unit One into a glitzy visitor centre, tasting room and bar/restaurant which became the official 'front of house' for the Meantime brand. Hooky (with the help of his architect father) did an absolutely stellar job in overseeing that entire project. By the time we came to sell the business in 2015, we had a fantastic, smart, cool and contemporary public face at Blackwall Lane, which is still there to this day. My careful relations with the Maritime Museum paid off later on, when in 2018 they decided to give up Units Two and Three and Meantime was able to move into them because I'd already negotiated a deal with the museum for when they chose to leave.

For the four years, then, from arriving at Meantime in Greenwich to signing the papers in 2015 to sell the company to SAB Miller, there was a relentless pressure to keep everything moving in the right direction and at the same time deal with unexpected problems along the way. That's the role of the leader, to ensure that everyone is able to deliver their best, that they're encouraged and enabled. Sometimes I liken this to the old fairground game when you have a wooden mallet and your task is to whack the head of every mole that springs up out of the ground in a bewildering variety in front of you. You get a great sense of satisfaction when you whack a mole and down he goes, only then to see another of the little tikes pop up over to the left. Leadership sometimes is all about playing whack-a-mole, about removing every obstacle as soon as it shows its head. Bang. Bang. Whack that mole, and clear the path so that the organisation you're leading can continue on the journey you've set them upon.

I had my own personal issues too: I'd moved to Meantime

while still married and in the early days was heading back to Newbury every weekend but in retrospect, it was clear that my marriage was coming to an end. By 2012 we had agreed to separate and I began to encourage the kids to come to visit me. They were old enough by then, George the youngest at 13, with Sam 16 and Annie a very grown-up 19. Sam and Annie were old enough to come and do work experience with me, which was great fun. I threw Sam onto the bottling line where he worked for the Albanian legend who was Bash, a mightily strong fellow who ruled the bottling area like a king. In fact, at one point, he had Sam stack up crates to form a throne so that he, Bash, could preside over his empire with authority. Annie, meanwhile, turned out to be a skilful barista and helped us out in the Old Brewery bar during the hectic time of the London Olympics in 2012, when Greenwich became the temporary home of the world's finest equestrians. George, although he was the youngest, braved his way to me alone from Newbury across London by Tube, and in 2013 he and I went skiing with Hooky, who was a gracious, patient and encouraging teacher, improving George's technique no end; it was such a pleasure for me to see the two of them get on so well.

Another thing happened to me during those turbulent years: I got together with Em, my beautiful wife. She'd moved to Greenwich in connection with her work, and was separated from her husband with her two girls, Alice and Izzy (the latter came to work for Meantime at The Old Brewery), who were of much the same age as my children. We courted for two years and in 2015, just before the Meantime sale, we bought a house in Greenwich and Em and I married. The kids all get on well, so much so that in 2014 we all went skiing together to Les Alpes d'Huez, with some of the kids bringing their own partners. It was great fun and since then all of us have grown into being part of an extended, integrated family.

I discovered, however, that leadership does involve a certain amount of loneliness. The people in your team want you to be the person who holds everything together because that gives them confidence, so I never confided much of my personal life at the time. I'm probably more of a get-on-with-it sort of person anyway. And there was always the potential for some disaster to derail the Meantime plans so I could never have the luxury of speculating on my own life too much. The Olympics in 2012 proved quite troublesome: we were expecting a huge uplift in sales in and around Greenwich which oddly didn't materialise and, instead, we found ourselves locked in petty disputes with other retailers, particularly around The Old Brewery pub we leased in the centre of Greenwich. One particular woman, who shall remain nameless, consistently shut the gates to The Old Brewery pub so she could divert the public to her own bar nearby, which ended up in a kind of ludicrous scenario of us chasing each other around The Old Brewery, one shutting the gates, the other re-opening them. Such is the glamorous life of craft beer.

More dangerous to us was when one of our customers, a pub in the centre of London, reported that a drinker had found some glass in the bottom of their bottle of Meantime. This is the kind of news which will turn you cold with fear: could it be that an entire batch of our beer had been damaged; would we be obliged to recall all the beer currently on sale in London and tip it down the drain? That could have had a massive impact on our carefully managed cash flow and, more importantly, our reputation. It's a very different situation when you're brewery owned and covered by a big PLC with access to treasury funds; I knew we had to get to 2015 without trying to raise any further funds so we had to work within our means. Thankfully, the problem turned out to be an isolated one, or maybe even a one-off attempted fraud, so we could breathe out again.

I was always very aware that I had left the security of a PLC with all the assets that I had at my disposal as a country manager for SAB Miller. When working there, any slight potential issue with an individual could be telegraphed up to human resources and an army of highly qualified people would be all over it like a rash, working out the most effective solution for all. When you're a bunch of fired-up individuals working to a limited budget in a brewery in Greenwich, you don't have that luxury. When £1000 was stolen from our safe upstairs at The Old Brewery pub, I had my suspicions who was behind it but if I'd pursued them, it could have shaken the confidence of the team, so I just dealt with the issue very quietly in my own way. There were allegations coming in at one point that drugs were being dealt in the vicinity of our pop-up bar on the South Bank outside the Festival Hall and that was the very last kind of publicity we needed, so before long we shut the outlet down.

The pubs themselves, the two pubs I inherited when I arrived in 2011 – The Greenwich Union and The Old Brewery – were managed in what I can only describe as an enthusiastic manner. Remember, I'd spent a chunk of time in the old days managing not two but 18 roughhouse pubs in north-east London ('meantime moments' again), so there weren't many tricks I didn't know how to spot. I was uncomfortable about some of the regular drinkers I saw at the Union but just kept my eye on them. As the theft from the Old Brewery safe demonstrated, I needed to keep my eye on the staff too. When I arrived, the two pubs combined were making us £400,000 if we were lucky; within two years, we had them making £800,000, with no real increase in turnover. It was all about not taking your eye off the ball, focusing on strategy, and implementing the One Per Cent Rule (Chapter Four). I was always nervous about Hooky's predilection for serving oysters in The Old Brewery with his porter: he insisted, I'm sure quite rightly, that they were a perfect match. But I knew that just one gyp-y tummy after eating our oysters would be trouble, and when we did finally have a case of food poisoning, I took them off the menu completely and replaced them with lobster, which ended up twice as profitable.

In those early days, I was tough on one character, Andy Ward, who had been one of the Meantime mainstays in the company's early days. Andy was and is a good man, but he struggled with my leadership style, particularly as I came down hard on what I saw as the inefficiencies of the operations at The Old Brewery. He was close to his staff and, in a way, too close because in my view he found it tough to make demands of them. He chose to move away to set up his own pub with a celebrity chef. My own take on this was that our brand, Meantime, was too important for any one individual to attempt to impose their own style of management: we all had to row with the same energy and the same rhythm; we had to show Meantime as a company that was much bigger than any one of its component parts, me and Hooky included. I have a few regrets that Andy wasn't able to stay with us and reap the rewards of the sale because he had been very instrumental in Meantime's story, but we were on a mission and couldn't afford to make exceptions in management style.

I remember one morning feeling one of those chill winds down my back when I was informed that a protest was taking place outside The Old Brewery. It turned out that a group of women who had attended one of our brewery tours the previous evening weren't happy and were registering their complaint, extremely vocally. Our brewery tours were magnificent, particularly once we'd upgraded Unit One to feature a glistening visitor centre and bar. We were seeing hundreds of people a week paying £15 each to be shown around the brewery, inspect the tanks and then enjoy a tasting session at the end. Our most charismatic guide, Big Al – a part-time stand-up comedian – had, according to these protesting ladies, used an unfortunate phrase to welcome them the previous evening, and all of them came from a female-only beer appreciation club. Knowing Big Al, who was a comedian at heart, and knowing his big heart inside that big frame of his, I knew instantly that he hadn't meant to give offence but that was irrelevant; we couldn't afford the kind of negative publicity that his turn of phrase might generate. I immediately headed down to The Old Brewery, apologised profusely and invited all the members of the club to come back the following week for a tour personally led by Rod Jones and me. They were gracious in accepting our apology, and no more came of it. But in this new era of social media, just one unforeseen incident like that could have a devastating effect.

Even celebrity TV chefs managed to cause us the odd problem. One of them, who shall remain nameless, failed to pay our invoice for the beers we supplied his new restaurant to the tune of £20,000 when, without warning, he liquidated his company. Again, I didn't need a public spat with a celebrity, so we swallowed the loss.

Some of the poor pigs who were fed our spent grain down in Kent weren't so lucky. Unbeknown to us, one of our trainee brewers had accidentally put the spent yeast in with the spent grain. Hooky got a call from the farmer:

'Alastair, I think we've got a problem with your spent grain.'

'What's that then?'

'I think there's yeast in it.'

'There shouldn't be. How do you know?'

'Well, two of my pigs have just exploded.'

Hooky had to spend £900 a piece on two new pigs for our farmer and we put in a few improvements into our brewery floor systems.

Despite these setbacks – and of course, they kept coming, which is what life will teach you – we were working well as a team and I was constantly adapting my 'PLC' mentality to life in a small business. Where possible, I would bring in better systems, always aware of the plan to have the business in shape to sell. I called on a human resources consultant from my days at Coors, Donna Branson, to come in and overhaul our pretty non-existent personnel systems. I knew by now how crucial recruiting is to a business and how intrinsic it is too to leadership: one of the most obvious points about effective leadership is knowing when you don't know something, and the way to deal with that in an organisation is to select effectively someone who does know. Why, for example, did I bring in Rich Myers, a relatively junior marketing exec from SAB Miller, to run our marketing at Meantime? Well, because I, as a middle-aged bloke, didn't really have the instinctive knowledge of how our more youthful, metropolitan consumer base lived, and I needed someone like Rich who could combine having his finger on the pulse of our consumers with the ability to run and motivate a marketing team to follow his lead. Effective recruitment is the way a leader ensures that the gaps in his or her knowledge or experience is covered. So we put in, with Donna's help, rigorous recruiting standards which helped us avoid making mistakes. I'd learned this lesson at Miller Brands: on two occasions, I personally overruled the SAB human resources advice on the suitability of a candidate, convinced on both occasions that my gut instinct was right and their psychometrics were wrong. On both occasions, I was wrong and we had to let both people go.

I used what I'd learned from my career to date and used competence-based criteria in all our recruitment situations. I'd look at the competencies we required for the job in question and would write three big, broad, open questions which applied specifically to each. So if I had five key competencies, I'd have 15 questions which I would ask in exactly the same way of every candidate. It's only in this way that you can keep the process on track, and not get sidelined by personal issues like whether or not the candidate likes cricket. You end up with a marked scorecard, and then and only then, if you've got two candidates with the same score, do you bring in other factors: I feel instinctively that this candidate will fit into our culture better than that one. Very quickly, we introduced this method of interviewing into the company so that everyone felt capable of applying it and we could claim to be consistent in our approach.

Working with Donna, we transformed the entire personnel system, which when I arrived consisted of little more than a welcome smile and a handshake. If businesses operate through a combination of people, time and money, then the first element, people, is by far and away the most important. Jack Welch, the charismatic head of General Electric, used what he called the 'Four Es' to describe the influence of people: how much Energy do they have, do they Energise those around them, do they have Edge, and are they able to Execute? (For more information on this, check his 2005 book *Winning*.)

We put in appraisal systems, goals, accountability structures, measurement systems, all the tried-and-tested human resource functions which actually exist not to catch people out, but to highlight when they do something right. A good appraisal provides a structure for the employee to gauge against his or her own personal roadmap. This is particularly important in the kind of rapidly growing environment we were creating because sometimes in those situations, a business can grow faster than an employee can keep up with: their capability can't keep up with the requirements of the business. One of the classic rubrics of human resources says this:

- Many people begin a job being unconsciously incompetent.

- They get a rude awakening when they realise consciously they are incompetent.

- Then, before long and with training and support, they aim to become consciously competent.

- Eventually, they can be unconsciously competent.

The ideal scenario is for your people to be consciously competent, and it's fair to say that almost everyone at Meantime had now reached that point, sufficiently conscious of their skills and ability to be able to function well, not so blasé that they forgot they were part of a team. What was also really important about this entire human resources overhaul was that, when we came to sell the business, we could demonstrate to our potential acquirer that we were a business running on clear and rational methodologies that would transfer easily into a bigger environment.

Gary Whitlie, now our non-executive director, became a constant source of sound accounting and commercial advice, helping out new finance director Bob Emms to set up the reporting systems in a way that both Gary and I knew would make the company more accessible to an incoming acquiring group. I recruited a new financial controller, Paul Robinson, who had impressed me when he worked on our accounts on behalf of our auditor, and together with Bob they made a really reliable team. Tony Carson, our board director and shareholder, was also of great value during this period in giving us strong advice on pub retailing.

Being in a small pond now rather than a big pool, it was easier in some ways to establish one-to-one relationships with people who could help us. The brewery at Blackwall Lane was an attractive and exciting place for people to visit and as we cleared up the space and got more efficiencies into the brewery, we saw more and more people coming down to pay us a visit. I had the pleasure of meeting the late Duke of Edinburgh and gave him a bottle of our cork-topped London Porter on board the Cutty Sark in Greenwich. When Denise Hyland took over as leader of Greenwich Council, we saw some real movement in key areas like planning permissions and traffic solutions: she was such a can-do supporter of local businesses that she made a point of listening to our concerns and taking effective action. Local MP Nick Raynsford always went out of his way to help us where he could. And already by 2012, there was a steady stream of large brewery owners whom I knew from my previous career making up pretexts to come and visit us: SAB Miller, Fuller's, Carlsberg, Coors… we had very senior executives from all these companies come for a wander round the brewery in 2012. Patrick Dardis from Young's took great pleasure in pulling a seven-iron out of my golf bag when he came to visit and went round the brewery whacking the big steel tanks to check how full they were. The dents are still there to this day. Throughout this period, Young's were of vital importance to us: they set the trends for the beer industry in London, no question of that, and to have them supporting us was a really massive advantage.

And we played hard too: in 2012 I sat at the back in the bow of a rowing boat on a journey from Chiswick to Deptford as part of the Thames Jubilee Regatta, with a fag in my mouth and the cox David Thompson repeatedly bellowing: 'Bow, watch your timing!' David sadly passed away in 2021 and the industry went to great lengths to salute one of their finest. As chair of Marston's he was hugely influential in transforming the company into one of the UK's biggest and most profitable brewing and pub groups.

The following year, Hooky and I joined four others for a coxed row across the English channel. We raised £40,000 for charity, I learned how to light a fag while still rowing, and I had blisters on my bum for weeks.

There was a sense of heightened activity which filtered through to everyone, partly because I'd been so clear that we were on a mission to change the face of British beer: everyone stepped up to the mark and wanted to be part of this journey. This sense of camaraderie I believe arose from the clarity of the mission. Everyone in the organisation by early 2012 knew that we were all focused on:

- **liquidity** – always making sure our cash position was tenable

- **capacity** – always ensuring we can make and bottle enough quality beer and deliver it on time to meet orders

- **sales** – always focusing on our route to market and key customers and providing a high-quality premium-priced offer

- **brand** – always building our authentic brand position and explaining it to our consumers and customers

- **retail** – always improving the performance of our pubs and pop-ups

- **capability** – always having the skills and tools for the task: people are the company's most important asset.

'Miller's Pillars', some people in the brewery called them. My task was to provide the leadership which would allow these six goals to be adopted by everyone and become part of everyone's daily work approach. We incorporated them into every weekly meeting, using them as the metric by which we judged our progress and made our decisions. We used them as a questioning tool when recruiting new colleagues. We never wavered from them.

Chapter Nine

Keep Your Foot on the Gas

I t was all systems go once we'd sorted the initial disasters about the potential EIS fund failure, and we wouldn't stop for the next four years. I had a clear strategic plan in my head and I knew that we wouldn't be able to afford to rest for a minute in delivering it. I'd arrived at Meantime in 2011 with plenty of knowledge about the brand's potential within the UK beer sector as a result of the in-depth analysis I'd done the previous year while still at SAB Miller. Put simply, that research demonstrated quite clearly that there was a market opportunity for a premium ale to follow on from the market success created by Peroni, a premium lager. Peroni had plenty of energy still to maintain its position as the dominant premium lager in Britain so there would have been little point in creating a competitor for it. But the Peroni story had shown that the consumer was open to upgrading his or her drinking experience if the product was of a high enough quality and presented in a convincing way; it had also shown that both manufacturer and retailer could benefit massively from the premium pricing which the brand platform allowed.

I knew that there was a consumer base out there which was open to this kind of premium experience and therefore at Meantime the first priority was to identify them: where were they? Where were they currently drinking? We had to forget about ourselves and our interests, and focus obsessively on our consumers. Once we'd done that and had begun to identify them, we could prioritise them: what were the locations and venues which would form our initial brand surge, our gold locations (see Chapter Seven)? Where would we then expand our sales into once we had succeeded, the silver locations? And what were the future brand expansion potentials, the bronze locations?

Our gold locations were all in London. London was the epicentre of interest in craft beer, interest in drinks experimentation, having sophisticated consumers with money to spend on lifestyle choices, many with a sincere interest in issues such as sustainability and localisation. London was our home and it was also where we had to build our brand. Having realised that, we began to break London down into areas of geographical interest. This time round, I wasn't interested in Mayfair; Peroni could keep the clubs of Berkeley Square. We wanted to dominate Shoreditch, Soho, London Bridge, Clapham, West London – the 'non-blingy' areas where you'd find consumers interested in expanding their knowledge of craft beer. These were areas with outlets dominated by Young's and Mitchells & Butlers so they were going to be our most important target customers. Once we'd identified where our consumers were drinking, then we could develop a brand proposition for our customers – the bars, restaurants and clubs – which would be beneficial to them.

We were going to operate a core marketing strategy which I'd used with my colleagues at Miller Brands: push and pull marketing. This is a vital concept to understand in any kind of consumer product marketing. Put simply, the pull element comes when you promote products directly at the consumer: you pull your consumer on to them. Now, this might be you doing that, or as the brand owner, you are more likely to be encouraging your retail customers to do that to the consumers they serve. If that's the case, then as the brand owner you support your retail customer by your role in push marketing: undertaking activities to attract consumers to your product so that they will either seek it out or will respond well when your retailer pushes it towards them. Again, you can't ever forget the features and benefits of your brand.

Push marketing can take various forms, from point of sale material[27] set up in the pub to special promotion nights where your beer is sampled. Perfume companies are always doing the latter: smartly dressed young women coming up to you in department stores and squirting perfume all over you. Essentially, push marketing is any kind of deliberate activity that will get your product into your consumer's hands. Pull marketing can often be more subtle and is a way of creating interest among consumers through, for example, experiential activities, sponsorship of like-minded events, word-of-mouth marketing campaigns, public relations and digital activities. As the brand owner, you need to be able to see both sides of this strategy coin, so that when you are going in to sell your

---

27 Point of sale material might include posters, cards, leaflets, competitions and so on.

product to your retailer, they understand that you are going to fulfil your side of the bargain in stimulating interest.

This is the crucial fact to remember: while we knew who our ideal consumers were, we couldn't actually talk to them straight away. In order to do that, we needed to talk to our customers, the retailers, who were the ones in a position to talk to the consumers. Brands can launch through consumer marketing, but it's often prohibitively expensive and they need to have a broad distribution already in place to make the expenditure worthwhile; most brands launch through trade marketing, and then they build on their initial success by gradually introducing more and more direct-to-consumer messaging. I've seen so many 'wannabe' brands fail because they thought their primary task was to talk direct to consumers and they forgot that their initial customer was the person serving the consumer. And when you're a small brand with potential like Meantime had in 2011, you actually don't want to make a big above-the-line consumer marketing noise because then you're going to put off the very people you're wanting to sign up: the consumers who want to feel they've 'discovered' you, who want to tell their friends about this amazing craft beer they've found. Those consumers will be put off if 'their' brand discovery is splashed all over the media – it's not their special find. (In the absence of a mature distribution programme, you would inevitably also be marketing to empty shelves.)

So our strategy – to create, build, expand – depended absolutely on the strength of the relationships we established with what we termed our 'gold' customers, the bar and pub chains of London. Let's take a look at what we had in our favour as an ambitious craft beer, compared with the traditional cask ales which consumers were offered at the bar:

1. Meantime was a keg beer, so it could be stored for longer than cask ale. That's a logistics 'plus' for a retailer.

2. Once the keg was opened at the pub, it would last for a week, whereas most cask ales would only last three or four days before turning bad, so the retailer would have much less wastage.

3. The retailer has got a distinct consumer benefit to offer: our beer is more consistent in quality because it's in a keg and it's served colder, which we know consumers like more and more.

4. We delivered our beer to our retailers with a beautiful new branded glass designed by Ian Cassie, who'd done all that work for me at Peroni. Another benefit much appreciated by the consumer as he or she lifted the pint to their lips.

5. We provided our retailers with a hugely attractive brand marketing message to pass on to the consumer: Meantime is a brand new concept; it's not the same old same old British beer. This is exciting craft beer, a totally new consumer proposition.

6. Last but by no means least, we could demonstrate to the retailer that every pint of Meantime sold in this way, as an exciting new craft beer, could be sold for £1 more than every other ale on the bar, thereby increasing the retailer's cash margin with every pint.

On that last point, let's look a little more closely at how the numbers worked. Let's assume that a pub chain was used to buying a barrel of beer from a brewer for £70 ex-duty. A barrel would contain 288 pints (the traditional British beer industry still talks in terms of barrels and firkins,[28] whereas the global beer market talks in hectolitres). So my conversation with the retailer would go something like this:

'You're paying £70 per barrel for beer, yes?'

'Yes.'

'I'm going to sell you a barrel of Meantime for £150.'

'Oh no you're not.'

'I am, and please listen to my argument. You're going to sell my Meantime for £1 a pint more than that other beer. That's £288 you've made. Take off the VAT, you've made circa £240. Take off the additional £80 you had to pay me, and you're still making £160 more in profit with every barrel you sell.'

I knew this conversation could work because at Peroni I'd convinced one pub group to shift from Stella to Peroni and over a period of three years they sold 20,000 barrels of Peroni at a pound a pint more than they'd sold Stella, giving them an additional EBITDA[29] contribution of over £1 million. If you begin to think about the performance of a big pub group and you consider how an addition of £1 million in EBITDA profit could result from just switching from one lager to another, then you can see just how crucial

---

28 A hogshead is 54 gallons, a barrel is 36 gallons, a kilderkin is 18 gallons, a firkin is 9 gallons, a polypin is 4.5 gallons.

29 Earnings before interest, tax, depreciation and amortisation: this is one metric for analysing a company's financial performance, used as an alternative to net income, which is the income into the company after cost of sales and overhead are stripped out.

this whole trade marketing/pricing matrix is when you're the brand owner. You've developed something which can have a massive and immediately positive impact on your customer's profit and loss account.

This, then, is classic route-to-market methodology. One of the rules of that methodology, which I'd spent much of my career learning, is that you never allow any of your key customers, your retailers, to hold more than ten per cent of your output. Because if for whatever reason you lose that customer, and they account for more than ten per cent, you'll never be able to replace the lost volume quickly enough to recover your financial position. So one of the many plates I had to keep spinning was the task of constantly checking that we weren't overexposed to any one customer. When you get an outstanding customer, as Young's proved to be for Meantime, it's tempting to ignore that rule, but I was always conscious that my aim was to sell the business, and for that reason I was strict about spreading our distribution across a number of retailers.

Once I'd recruited Melanie Smith to come and join us as sales director and had Rich on board, we were able to begin building this trade marketing programme because I knew I could rely on them both to implement the plan that had been drawn up and also to manage a growing team of salespeople. So while I might be the one to commence negotiations with people like Mitchells & Butlers, as I had long-standing relationships with them, Mel and her team were more than capable of handling and delivering the ensuing relationship while at the same time bringing in new customers. The same applied to all our trade customers: we brought in pub group Stonegate working closely there with Ian Payne, Suzanne

Baker and David Just; we secured Enterprise Inns through an existing friendship with boss Simon Townsend and we brought in Davy's Wine Bar, having known James Davy through the regional brewer days. The Young's relationship was handled brilliantly by Harry, our floppy-haired, heartthrob young salesman; Matthew Macaloon joined us and did a superb job with SSP Group, a heavy provider of catering services at travel outlets. Ben Joseph, meanwhile, brought in a fine collection of more eclectic customers, really useful streetwise outlets in the East End and South London which did the same job of bringing us consumers. Rob Hacker dealt with a number of our original customers and also oversaw the export market.

By focusing initially on trade marketing, we were able to generate momentum swiftly and we didn't swerve from our commitment to ensuring that our gold customers – the bar and pub groups of London – were consistently treated with respect and determination. Here was our proposition to our retail customers: can we build the transaction and make you more money? Can you make more profit with every pint you sell? That's what is known as transaction building. Second, can we attract the consumer on your behalf, encourage them to come into your pub? (This is called driving footfall.) That's a slightly more nebulous claim to prove, but we did know that more and more consumers were actively seeking out craft beer. The newness of the storytelling enhanced the image of beer to our consumers. Last but not least, image: does our image enhance the image of your pub?

We went to each and every one of them with a profitable and attractive solution: stock Meantime beer, and your customers will enjoy the consumer experience while you will enjoy the profit benefit. There was never any doubt in our sales pitch: we assure you, this will work. And it did. By the time we came to sell the business in 2015, the on-trade accounted for 83 per cent of our sales; even in calendar year 2014, we added 450-plus new on-trade accounts to the business to continue the growth swing. And of our entire on-trade customer base, by 2015 the top ten customers accounted for just over 50 per cent of our total sales, virtually a textbook spread of retail customer accounts.

As far as the off-trade was concerned, I took the decision early on that we couldn't operate successfully across all sectors with such a small sales team. So all our focus remained on the on-trade, where we did remarkably well, and I allowed us to pick up whatever off-trade opportunities came our way. Hooky had previously done well with the Sainsbury's Taste the Difference range, but I didn't want our on-trade focus to be diluted by something similar. The BrewDog boys had stolen a march on the off-trade and were doing very well in supermarkets, so I was happy just to see our bottles being stocked in Marks & Spencer, Waitrose and Majestic. I've never believed that you can really build a beer brand by relying on the off-trade, because to this day I've never seen a supermarket provide a consumer with the experiential engagement with a brand which a pub can give you. So by 2015, the off-trade accounted for just ten per cent of our turnover and that suited me just fine. It meant we hadn't diverted our attention from the much more significant (in terms of brand-building) on-trade, and it also provided me with another premium benefit to offer when selling the company: look how much scope there is to expand into the off-trade range of supermarkets!

Exactly the same principle applied to export, run for us expertly by Rob Hacker. By 2015, another 10 per cent of our turnover came from export sales and I never even worried about setting up a big export sales department. In fact, what we did do was to bring in the few export sales we achieved in territories like Italy and Holland because I knew by dipping the Meantime toe into those waters, we would get the attention of SAB Miller who were strong in both markets. Again, I was thinking about the most effective way to build the business swiftly, which meant focusing all our sales attention on the on-trade in London: exports and the off-trade were proven markets; they were just unexploited by us at that stage. We were going to sell this business: why not stimulate interest early on? And then when we came to sell it, we had the off-trade at ten per cent and export at ten per cent, and I was able to say to our potential acquirer: just run the numbers on the impact you'll make by expanding both of those using your own off-trade and export sales teams.

While building this trade marketing strategy and bringing in Mel to head up a rapidly growing sales team, I was also building our marketing profile as quickly as possible. We hired Maureen Heffernan, the highly experienced trade PR executive who had worked for Miller Brands on the Peroni brand, and once again she did a cracking job this time on the Meantime brand. I've mentioned that I recruited a brand manager from Miller Brands UK, Rich Myers, and brought him in on promotion as marketing director. Together we began to map out the kind of vigorous marketing profile which our on-trade sales strategy required to support it. I gave Rich a specific brief: I wanted him to market to himself, as he was the epitome of our target consumer. Ian Cassie was signed up to implement the creative strategy and before long had transformed the graphics on the Meantime logo, introduced new fonts and designed a fabulous set of glassware for us to offer our pub customers, which not only looked beautiful but had design benefits for the consumer: the Meantime ale glass opened out at the top to allow the drinker to smell the aroma as he or she raised the glass to their lips, whereas the Meantime lager glass was more tulip shaped to retain the carbonation and therefore the consistency of the head. These kinds of details were just what our sophisticated consumers liked to hear. Before long, we had given Meantime the very cool, semi-industrial chic look: not a brass tap in sight anywhere, just cool steel edges all designed to appeal to our metropolitan, 'hipster' core clientele and to give the brand a premium feel.

Ian, by the way, was and remains to this day a really influential figure within UK product and branding design. He's always involved in the most interesting work. At one point, one of our Meantime shareholders called me up and asked if I could help find some work experience for his next door neighbour's teenager. These are always quite onerous obligations to take on because inevitably they involve a fair amount of admin, but most of us are happy to help the next generation so I agreed to take her on for two weeks. Rich Myers took her under his wing for a week in the marketing department, and for the second I persuaded Ian to give her a week's experience at his agency, Black Arts. Ian's only proviso was that she had to be prepared to make tea. On her first day with him, he asked her to prepare four teas and bring them into his office. She did so, knocked on the door, brought in the tray and gave the tea out to actors Michael Douglas, Robert De Niro and Samuel L. Jackson, plus Ian. Cassie had developed a creative concept called Love the Glove to support the work of the health service in combating prostate cancer, and all three men had agreed to feature in the film he was making. What a memory associated with work experience that young woman would have had! If I'd have known, I'd have gone to make the tea.

We didn't have the budget for a massive advertising campaign, and as I've already mentioned, a brand like Meantime didn't want to be operating in that blatant fashion anyway. We were much cooler than that – we were the desirable London craft beer that we were going to enable our consumers to 'discover'. We ran just one advertising campaign early on, a £30,000 'Londoner' campaign on posters in the London Underground, and in some senses I approved that because I wanted to send out a message to the beer industry: we're serious about introducing craft beer to the market. What we did do, however, was some fabulous and innovative marketing campaigns which Rich and his team delivered with panache. There were some really effective and committed people working for Rich: Andrew Hall, cousin of footballer Ian Wright, developed all of our trade marketing tools for our sales force; Maddie Blackall did a faultless job running our consumer marketing and social media activities; Alec Fleming organised a lot of our capital build concepts like the beer vans, pop-ups and festival lorries, and was absolutely fantastic throughout. In fact, that whole experiential marketing work which we conducted and which was implemented through Alec's installations was a crucial part of the Meantime marketing success, a classic example of pull marketing working effectively.

Another of Rich's team's most effective and inspiring pull ideas was the Hops in a Box campaign which we launched in April 2013, for which we sited 12,500 hop-growing kits across 100 of our customer outlets in London to encourage consumers to grow hops. What we were doing here was drawing attention to the natural quality of the ingredients in Meantime beer and encouraging consumers to engage in the process of how it was made. As a marketing campaign, it hit all our targets beautifully: the boxes were usually close to the point of purchase of our beer; they were perfect content for the digital world, with consumers taking photos of themselves growing hops in different environments; it was perfect in an experiential sense because our consumers were actually playing with one of the core ingredients of our beer and it was massively PR-able, particularly when we launched our Greenwich Hop Garden down on the Peninsula. We tried to ensure that every marketing campaign we conducted hit those four targets, but I don't think any campaign struck as sweet a note in that respect as Hops in a Box. I had learned that, in any marketing campaign, there are really only nine marketing propositions you can make – national pride, local pride, luxury, does what it says on the tin, health, quality, heritage, community/charity, environmental – and that in any campaign you can really only focus on two before you start confusing the consumer. We focused on local pride and quality.

In fact, I trusted Rich so much that I respected his request that I keep my nose out of his team creative meetings: he said that, as the boss, I'd cast too great a shadow over meetings and stifle creativity. Too much the 'bad cop' in the room. If the results are anything to go by, he was right. I took that line too when it came to a big industry awards ceremony which had shortlisted Hops in a Box in a number of marketing categories. Not wanting to steal Rich's thunder, I told him I wasn't going to the swanky ceremony in Park Lane, and that he would represent Meantime. That evening, as I sat at home, I kept getting messages from him as, one after the other, his campaign was awarded prize after prize, eventually finishing the night with a real haul of six wins. I couldn't have been happier, my delight increased by the knowledge that Rich had been recognised for his role in person.

One of our most successful marketing campaigns emerged, you'll not be surprised to hear, on the golf course. It was early in 2013 and Hooky and I were having one of our usual contests. He was probably winning, and I mentioned to him that while I'd been running Miller Brands, we'd been thinking of introducing the idea of tanked beer for the Pilsner Urquell brand as a way of giving it a market differential. Tanked beer used to be a staple of the British keg scene in the 1970s, when beer consumption was much higher than it is now. In order to save costs and also boost freshness, a busy bar like the Punch and Judy in London's Covent Garden would have a great big, plastic-lined cellar and every so often a tanker would come along and a fellow would stick a hose into the cellar and fill it up. No more stacks of metal barrels, no more changing of the barrel mid-order, no more worries about freshness – this was fresh from the brewery.

As British consumers began to drink less beer from the 1980s on, tanked beer got phased out and pretty much forgotten about. But in big beer-drinking markets like Germany and the Czech Republic, it never went away, and I'd visited a number of very popular Czech bars where Pilsner Urquell was served from tanks. The consumer is delighted, too, because he or she is assured that the beer they're drinking is fresh from the brewery, is unfiltered, naturally carbonated, unpasteurised and generally as close to perfect beer as you can get.

So I was chatting with Hooky, trying to put him off his stroke, and I told him how at SAB we couldn't proceed with the plan because the logistics of bringing tankers over to the UK from the Czech Republic and then splitting them up around the UK was just not economic. Hooky looked up from his putter.

'We could do it, though,' he said. 'We could absolutely do that.'

A week later, he and I flew to Holland and purchased the brewery equivalent of a petrol pump, a dispensing unit which we had delivered to Greenwich and fitted to a massive tanker. Among all of us – Hooky overseeing the beer, Ben looking after the logistics, Mel talking to the customers and Rich coming up with the marketing collateral, with Bob sorting out the finance and me keeping the ship on course – we launched Meantime Brewery Fresh in March 2013 in association with Young's at three of their pubs: the Plough in Clapham, the Grove in Balham and the Windmill, also in Clapham. Mel, Harry and I had persuaded Young's to install a decent-sized tank in each of these three pubs. The tanks cost us about £9000 per pub, but again, we crafted it well to give us benefit: it was a capital purchase for us so this was a depreciating cost on our balance sheet, and didn't hit our profit and loss. The launch was an immediate success, with all the marketing benefits of brewery-fresh craft beer made obvious to the customer right there on the bar. We were assuring Young's customers that the beer remains unpasteurised and unfiltered, and therefore continues to mature in tank and actually improves even while it's in the outlet. Brilliant! The process also meant the beer had no contact with the air until it hit the glass (compressed air used in traditional dispensing can adversely affect the taste and ultimately the quality of the beer). Rich's marketing campaign made clear that a pint of Meantime Brewery Fresh was like drinking a beer direct from the brewery itself, as fresh as the day it was made.

Eventually we had Brewery Fresh installed in 25 outlets around London. We had national press coverage, we had the beer writers congratulating us on bringing authenticity to the bar and talking excitedly about the 'tanknova' or tank pubs of Prague. Most importantly, we had created that sense of experiential enjoyment which we needed our key London gold consumers to feel and to pass on to their friends. Not a single person mentioned that we were in fact resurrecting the way beer had often been delivered to working men's clubs in the 1970s: our marketing was precise and confident about bringing over from our Continental friends the means by which London drinkers could drink better beer. As Hooky gleefully explained to journalists: 'The beer is so fresh it's like having a microbrewery in the pub.' And the manager of the Grove in Balham, one of our earlier Brewery Fresh outlets, gave us the perfect endorsement in the pages of the *Evening Standard*: 'It sells itself,' he said. 'It's been the number one drink for the last two weeks.'

Everything about the Brewery Fresh campaign hit our sweet spots. With one or two stubborn exceptions, we persuaded our targeted customers to store the beer in sleek steel tanks at their venues which the consumers could see, thus reaffirming the cool, trendy Meantime feel. We put a big stainless steel tank outside the National Theatre on the South Bank and filled it with Brewery Fresh. Then, we began to take the beer out to festivals – British Summer Time in Hyde Park, Love Box in Victoria Park, Pride – and the big sleek stainless steel Meantime tanker became a real draw, attracting craft beer aficionados but also new audiences wherever we went.

Then we came upon an opportunity to host our own bar closer to home, outside the O2 venue on Greenwich Peninsula. Rich and Alec had been trying for a while to set up a cool Meantime bar using shipping containers at the Box Park in Shoreditch, a trendy collection of designer shops outside Shoreditch Tube station which were all housed in shipping containers. This would have been another great place to showcase Brewery Fresh lager, but we couldn't get a reasonable enough rent agreed so we had walked away from the deal. We had a ready-made plan with nowhere to install it, so I suggested to Rich that we pitch it to the owners of the land around the old Millennium Dome, the O2 venue, which was by now one of the most successful music venues in London. I knew the owners (a Chinese corporation called Knight Dragon) needed to deliver positive PR about how they were working well with the local community because they were keen to see their planning proposals accepted by the council, so we pitched the Meantime shipping container bar idea to them as a way of them giving support for local business. The pitch went even better than I could have hoped. Not only did they say yes, but they volunteered to buy the containers for us. Just for fun, I suggested a rent deal to them which would reduce our rent the more beer we sold; normally, you'd expect it to work the other way, but they liked the idea of backing Greenwich so much they agreed. To be fair, I'd invested a fair amount of time going out and about in Greenwich, getting to know key people like MP Nick Raynsford and council leader Denise Hyland, both of whom were really supportive of Meantime, and I think that link with them was also perceived as being valuable by the O2 property owners.

Alec Fleming started doing his magic again and fitted out the three shipping containers so that one was the servery area, the second was the bar and the third was the cellar. We built a roof garden on top of it with an umbrella which kept blowing off in the wind, and we launched it with a surprise gig by the band We Are Scientists playing on the roof. We called it the Beer Box and Hooky brewed an exclusive beer, the Peninsula Pale Ale, which of course we delivered using the Brewery Fresh tanker. With the massive flow of people in and out of concerts at the O2, we were taking £10,000 per week with very little rent and hardly any infrastructure or staff costs. In its first year, it delivered £100,000 profit to Meantime, on an outlay of just £40,000. But probably more valuable to us was the marketing impact: every week, thousands and thousands of London consumers would come out of the North Greenwich Tube station onto Millennium Square and begin to head towards the O2, where they were excited about seeing their favourite band. And right in front of them, written out in big fluorescent letters, was Meantime. And let's not forget the non-Londoners who had come into the capital for a big night out at the O2 – they would be taking our brand message back to their friends outside of

London, priming the rest of the UK for future marketing approaches.

All these marketing activities, from Hops in a Box to the Beer Box, Brewery Fresh to the event lorries, were either of minimal cost to us or, as was the case with the Beer Box and the event lorries, actually delivered revenue. But primarily they were marketing tools, offering savvy London consumers the chance to engage with our brand, to spread the word, to reassure our on-trade customers that our brand was growing and to spread the word among the big beasts of the beer industry that Meantime was making some serious waves. Our vision was to change the way that London consumers felt about beer by pioneering innovative campaigns; all these marketing programmes were targeted specifically to allow those consumers to engage directly with the brand and to feel that it could be a part of their lifestyle. If we were going to achieve my minimum target, that of selling the business for £50 million, we needed to prove to any prospective buyer that in a world where craft beer was rapidly becoming the 'next big thing' (in America, the original home of craft beer, the sector had already expanded to 15 per cent of the total US beer market, and the UK generally followed American beer trends), Meantime represented the most desirable brand. BrewDog was complicated in many ways by its crowdfunding structure and its very aggressive marketing attitude, and our only other rival, Camden, had done very well but hadn't managed to achieve the growth levels we did in four years; I knew we had to out-innovate them. We had worked our socks off to give Meantime a genuine, authentic sense of being a crafted beer, made in London from excellent ingredients by men and women passionate about brewing, which would always be a reliable and profitable supplier to pub chains like Young's and Enterprise and all the others.

Our growth was exactly how I wanted it. Between 2011 and the end of 2012, we grew our brewing turnover by 60 per cent and increased the group's EBITDA by almost 30 per cent. The following year, 2013, our brewing was 40 per cent up, with beers like our London Lager, London Pale Ale, Yakima Red and Pilsner all trading 100 per cent up year on year. A year later, the accounts for the end of 2014 showed another 45 per cent group turnover increase and a staggering 95 per cent increase in our EBITDA to £2.5 million. These explosive advances were effectively based on the One Per Cent Rule I had first learned back in the days of Bass Taverns running 18 pubs: by increasing turnover and controlling costs, you begin to get overhead recovery and thereby exponential profit growth.

By this stage, we were all working so well as a team that even my never-ending catchphrases and mottoes ('Miller's Pillars') were treated almost affectionately by my colleagues. When I wanted us to obsess about the integrity of our brand, I'd talk about the snowball, how as it rolls down the hill it gathers more and more substance and increases its weight until eventually it becomes unstoppable. When I wanted people to stick to the task they had been allocated and not keep trying to come up with solutions for other departments, I referred to meerkats – Ben Joseph, in his endlessly energetic desire to see us win, was a prime example, and I'd bring him back a plastic meerkat from the garage and plonk it on his desk every time I thought he was letting his enthusiasm run away with him. It became a funny, affectionate joke between us. When a task seemed too big to contemplate, I'd tell them that the way to eat an elephant was in bite-sized chunks: only chew off what you can digest. Sometimes, businesses can fail because of what the consultants call 'cultural disconnect': when the employees aren't on the same wavelength as the leadership. By introducing some humour into our processes and my fixed vision, I think I found ways of making sure we felt like a unified team.

We kept on winning awards, with Hooky energised like never before to craft amazing brews. His Raspberry Wheat Beer won silver in the World Beer Cup; London Pale Ale won silver in the International Beer Challenge; London Lager, Pilsner, Yakima Red, Coffee Porter and London Porter all won bronze in the International Beer Challenge. In 2014 alone, our brewers produced over 40 different varieties of beer with our flagship brand, London Pale Ale, growing in volume by 78 per cent in 2014.

In 2014, we won Business of the Year in the London Business Awards. Our marketing campaigns won Campaign of the Year in the 2014 Digi Awards as well as a host of other awards. We were selected as one of the *Sunday Times* Fast Track 100 'Companies to Watch', and we won the HSBC Global Connections award for London and the South-East, securing a £150,000 prize into the bargain.

Ultimately, though, as with many things in life, it's all about the timing, and now maybe it was time to sell. You reap what you sow.

Chapter Ten

The Sale

I'd done my level best as managing director at SAB Miller in 2010 to persuade them to buy Meantime. It was a no-brainer: SAB Miller should have tried to buy it then and probably could have done for somewhere in the region of £10 million to £15 million. Instead, five years later, they had to pay the price for a company that was on a roll. As our American friends say: go figure. So when Creepy dared me to jump off the corporate diving board and come and run Meantime, I did so with the clear intention of coming in to build the business and sell it. That was what the senior shareholders made clear they wanted and that also suited all the investors who had come into the business under the EIS rules; their tax benefits would end after three years and they'd be hoping to see a return on their investment so they could take a stake in another business. That's one of the key things to remember when accepting investment under EIS rules: your shareholders won't necessarily want to stay with you forever – they will be hoping for a profitable exit and then another adventure. It was clear when I took the job at Meantime that I was working for the shareholders.

In my head, as I looked around that scruffy office and the wallpaper-pasting desk in September 2011, I had the figure of £50 million in mind. That would give a reasonable return to all investors, it would reward the staff, it would reward me; everyone would benefit. That seemed like a not excessively ambitious goal, and I gave myself five years to achieve it: five years to turn the business around and make it attractive enough for someone to splash £50 million on it. Everything I did from that point on was done with that objective in mind: I began selling Meantime in September 2011. The way I did that was to ensure that every decision I took would benefit us when it came to a sale. Was I worried about creating too much brewing capacity at the Greenwich brewery? No, because I knew I wanted to show a prospective buyer that the business could upscale even more with their backing behind it. Was I concerned about not really building sales with the off-trade supermarkets like Sainsbury's? No, because again that left an opportunity for an incoming buyer to exploit. I had also been deliberately strategic in my approach to the press ever since I'd arrived, positioning Hooky as the genius brewer that he was but also emphasising the broader team, the way in which we worked together, the innovations we kept on producing: I wanted the industry to see us as a coherent, well-organised business that could survive an acquisition intact. I didn't want press focus on any one individual, just the beer and the team. The beer and the team, that was all we would show.

During 2014, however, a few incidents made me realise that my original time frame of five years might be too long and that it might be 2015 rather than 2016 that ought to be my focus for the sale. Sometimes it's as important knowing when to get out of a situation as it is knowing when to get in. In the autumn of 2014, we had a semi-formal approach from a European family office (see note 19, Chapter Three). The figure was impressive but they would have wanted me and the key board members to stay on for at least three years. The Meantime board politely turned them down, but I knew that they were keeping an eye. Then Hooky's health took a dip and he began to make suggestions about retiring on a dividend stream from the business. This would have damaged our credibility and could have seen me obliged to stay in position for another chunk of time while I raised another brewer good enough to take over his role. I persuaded him to stay on as long as I accelerated the endgame. Then later in 2014, one of our senior shareholders let slip, while perhaps having imbibed one too many of Hooky's excellent beers, that I'd done what they'd wanted me to do back in 2011 and perhaps it was time to let me go before I was allowed to benefit too much from any potential sale. Not a smart remark to let someone like me pick up, obviously, but who knows: perhaps in retrospect it was done deliberately to put even more fire in me? I don't know to this day and I hold no grudge whatsoever, but it certainly made me think there was no time to lose.

Interestingly, I didn't really need to do that much: the stellar performance of the business in 2013 and 2014 meant that the big beasts of the British beer industry were already starting to hover over us. They all needed new products to differentiate themselves, and they were all nervous about missing out on the craft beer phenomenon. Quietly, they began to make visits and we were inspected under various different social pretexts by the great and the good of the beer world. I know for a fact that during 2014, Asahi and Estrella Damm and San Miguel all cast their eyes over us. At one point, even Michael Turner, the chairman of Fuller's, deigned to wander around our premises and said something flippant about how on a good day he might offer me £20 million for the business. I told him that his figure was probably out by about a hundred million pounds and he just laughed at me. Jonathan Neame, the chairman of Shepherd Neame, came to visit me to pay a social call and although we just spoke about the industry, I suspected he was taking a few surreptitious glances at Hooky's shiny steel tanks.

The first formal approach came on 16 December 2014 when Gary Whitlie and I were visited at the brewery by Mark Hunter and Gavin Hattersley, chief executive and finance director respectively of Coors, one of the biggest global brewers. Mark had taken over as CEO of Coors from Peter Swinburn and I knew him well; Gavin had previously been a board director at Miller Brands UK when we set it up. The conversation was jovial, with plenty of banter as was to be expected among old colleagues, but although nothing was offered and no numbers were discussed, it was obvious that they were taking a serious look at our business. This was the first real indication that the vultures were circling.

The second pointer came in early February 2015, when Gary and I were invited over to Copenhagen by Bruce Ray, who was corporate affairs director for Carlsberg UK at the time. I'd known Bruce for years and he'd already visited me at Meantime a year before, just paying a social call as it were. We had some pretty serious discussions about our business and were wined and dined in Copenhagen's finest restaurants, but we told the Carlsberg directors that it was too early for us to consider a sale; we wanted to continue our growth pattern for a while longer to demonstrate the power of the brand. Perhaps a little bit of reverse psychology in there, to instil a worry in them that if they couldn't acquire us now, they'd have to pay a lot more in 12 months.

In general, therefore, from the end of 2014 into early 2015, I was deliberately building a sense of competitive tension, dropping the odd hint here and there to industry bigwigs and ex-colleagues at SAB who I knew would pass it on. I never mentioned figures – I never even suggested Meantime might be for sale – but I just carefully allowed the odd remark to slip out, and it was clearly having an effect: my diary of the time shows a steady stream of industry figures coming down to Greenwich on a variety of pretexts. The business itself was operating at full steam, everyone at Meantime was playing at the top of their game, sales were continuing to rise every week. The fact the company was operating so well gave me the time to focus on my sale strategy and by February 2015 most decisions I took had this in mind (every member of the board was aware of and in support of what I was doing). By early March we all knew that we were heading towards a sale. We decided to conduct a beauty parade of advisors. When you're selling a company, you need an approved advisor to act on your behalf for the construction of the deal in terms of paperwork, due diligence and so on; working from your strategy and lead, they build the architecture of the deal. We looked at all the big firms in this area – Sapient, Nomura, Alix, Cavendish – and asked them to present to us with their idea of a valuation. They all came back to us with a valuation of between £50 million and £90 million, working from financial projections of future performance based on the current year's trading.

Let me just go into this a little more closely. Our audited accounts for the end of 2014 alone wouldn't have justified these kinds of figures. Although those accounts showed tremendous growth year on year from the previous two years, they showed a turnover of almost £17 million and a consolidated EBITDA of almost £2.5 million. If you looked at what the business was doing in 2011, that was very good going. But because we'd put in such durable and rigorous business systems across the board – from Mel's sales team to Rich's marketing campaigns, Hooky's brewing to Bob's financial controls – we were able to forecast future performance quite accurately. Growth to date had virtually all been in the London area; we hadn't really even touched the on-trade across the rest of the country, while exports and the off-trade remained nascent as I've mentioned. Our PR and marketing presence was absolutely sky high; we were the darlings of the craft beer sector, which most industry analysts forecast as being the key area of growth in British beer. With our careful management of space and use of capital funds, we had sufficient capacity at Blackwall Lane to double our brewing or even more. The forecasts indicated that we'd reach 100,000 hectolitres of beer sold within the next two years – remember, when I arrived and once I'd stripped out the conflicting BrewDog and Adnams contract brewing, we were selling a tenth of that. That would see our EBITDA quadruple and it was on that basis, forecasting future annual growth of around 35 per cent a year, that the advisors were setting the kind of target figures for an effective sale, basing their valuation on predicted growth rather than current sales.

On 4 March, the temperature suddenly got even higher when Andrew Woodhouse (who ran mergers and acquisitions – M&A – for SAB Miller) arrived in Greenwich asking to buy beer for his 50th birthday. I already knew Andrew pretty well from my days at Miller Brands; every now and then during my tenure as managing director there, he'd call me in to give an opinion on a brand they were considering, and I never ceased to be impressed by the massive security his M&A team worked under. When I used to go and see him, I had to stand outside their locked office and wait to be admitted; once a month, they swept the entire office to check for hostile recording devices. It was a seriously run operation. Tall, highly educated and a fine skier and all-round sportsman, Andrew was a formidable M&A specialist; there weren't many developments taking place within the industry that he didn't know about and scrutinised with that genial yet piercing intelligence. Suddenly, there he was at our Meantime brewery, asking to buy a few cases of Hooky's finest for his birthday party. I smiled, and without hesitating, said:

'Well, you can buy the whole lot if you want.'

We were off. In my heart of hearts, I'd always known that SAB Miller were going to be the perfect company to sell to. Four years after I'd left them, they still needed a premium craft ale to replicate the Peroni magic, and they knew like everyone else in the industry that craft beer was without question the most desirable sector of the beer market. I knew SAB Miller inside out, and I knew that Meantime would fit perfectly inside their structure. I had also read the rumours in the trade press that there was a much, much bigger deal on the horizon: allegedly a dataroom had been set up in the City of London for the global brewing colossus Anheuser-Busch InBev (ABI). A dataroom is a temporary holding place for highly confidential information to be collected in advance of a merger/acquisition deal. ABI was obviously looking seriously at making a big acquisition, and there was some growing trade press speculation that SAB Miller must be the target. If those rumours were correct, then it would make sense for Andrew to be looking to make a 'sexy' acquisition to bump up the value of SAB Miller at the early stages of the courting by ABI. This was all trade press speculation but when the £79 billion acquisition of SAB Miller by ABI was announced in October 2016, it was proved to be spot on.

Now we were moving very, very quickly. After Andrew's beer-buying visit, we had several conversations over the phone and then I met him a week later at a coffee shop in Waterloo station at 8.15 in the morning on 11 March. I laid out my terms on the understanding that he and SAB Miller would 'go exclusive': if he came in with a bid for Meantime, our board would only talk to him, not to any of his competitors. The purpose of giving him exclusivity was to leverage the highest price he could offer. He was well aware that groups like Carlsberg and Coors were circling, so by committing exclusively to him I was driving him to offer a knockout price. I said:

'Andrew, you've got to pay a premium for the exclusivity. Don't even bother if your initial offer doesn't have a 100 in front of it.' I thought to myself: go big, they can always say no.

I told Andrew that we wanted a deal done quickly, we didn't want massive due diligence (I assured him that I had been scrupulous in going over everything about the company over the previous four years to ensure it would be in perfect condition for an acquisition) and neither Hooky nor I as the two senior executive directors would be prepared to have too many onerous warranties[30] held over us, which could have led to penalties. He agreed and said he would consult with Domenic de Lorenzo, the incoming chief financial officer for the SAB Miller Group.

The next meeting took place a week later, on 20 March. Domenic de Lorenzo came down to Greenwich with Sue Clark, who ran Western Europe for the whole SAB Miller Group. I knew both of them from my days running Miller Brands UK. Sue had been a non-executive director of my board there. She was a massively experienced and successful global operator, and she'd done some very serious things like setting up an AIDS healthcare programme in Tanzania. Sue operated at the highest level – I remember she once invited me to join her for dinner with F.W. de Klerk, the former president of South Africa. I liked, trusted and respected her, as I did Dom. He was from Cape Town, South Africa, a highly driven, tough banker who always drove his team hard. Domenic was a powerful operator, never someone you'd underestimate, and he was always impeccably turned out in pinstripe suits and metal-rimmed glasses.

The Meantime board was now fully engaged with the sale process, and appointed a smaller team consisting of myself, Gary Whitlie and Ian Colletts in order to pursue the deal. We

---

30 In a commercial transaction such as a corporate sale, a warranty is a contractual statement of assurance given by the seller to the buyer that a certain state of affairs exists.

met with Andrew, Domenic and Sue at the Beer Box outside the O2 at 4.30 pm on Friday 20 March. As soon as Domenic arrived, I told him that we only had half an hour because Ian, being Jewish, would have to leave at 5 pm to get home for Shabbat. So, if they were serious about wanting to buy Meantime, they would have to make an offer in the next 30 minutes. Remember, at this point, neither Domenic nor Sue to my knowledge had even stepped foot inside the Meantime brewery, half a mile away.

The six of us sat down with a beer outside the Beer Box. I spoke first:

'You're going to have to make a sensible offer to these guys' – indicating Ian and Gary – 'or they're going to walk away. I'm not the majority shareholder of Meantime; I only have so much say in this. They represent the major shareholders; they don't have to sell the company.'

'Ninety million,' Domenic said.

Ian headed off home for Shabbat and Gary and I took the three of them over to Meantime to have their first look around. I showed them a series of notes I'd drawn up on each key area: off-trade, export, on-trade plans for outside of London, new product development, brewing capacity, cash flow forecasts. We went out for a decent dinner at The Old Brewery then all went our separate ways. The first serious offer had been made.

I got up the following morning at seven o'clock and then spent the entire weekend writing a detailed paper setting out exactly why Meantime was such a good fit for SAB Miller. In effect, I wrote their acquisition strategy for them. Without revealing my suspicions about the impending deal with ABI, I set out how the purchase of Meantime would make SAB

Miller a more attractive proposition in the marketplace. I also dropped some hints about the competitive threat to them of another group acquiring us, and of them therefore appearing to lose the craft beer race. I also suggested that the City of London would react positively to the news of an acquisition, boosting SAB Miller's Stock Exchange share price. Finally, this would enable them to have a brewery in their listed marketplace. The paper ended by stating that the initial offer of £90 million was too low and, in fact, disingenuous. I sent the paper to Ian and Gary on Sunday morning, they checked and approved it, and at 8 pm that Sunday I emailed it to Domenic de Lorenzo. I added a cheeky line into the email:

'I don't even know why you're spending any time worrying about this; you could buy us on your expense account alone!'

At one minute past nine the following morning, I receive an email. They have increased their offer to £105 million. Now I'm getting excited. The following day, Tuesday 24 March, I go to the SAB Miller plc offices in Mayfair with Ian Colletts. I go into the building with a coat over my head as I've worked there recently – it's absolutely vital that these negotiations are in secret and we can't let anyone in the SAB Miller organisation recognise me. The four of us – Ian and I, Domenic and Andrew Woodhouse – meet in the Grolsch Room on the first floor at 4 pm, and we go at it hammer and tongs. I'm being as provocative as I can, and for four hours we go round and round in circles. It's not enough, I keep telling them. Read the paper I sent you on Sunday, look at the arguments: it's not enough. But not one of the four of us in that room wants to get off the pot and make the final offer. We're skirting the issue. I keep on at them. I go through every department at Meantime, I show them once more how

I've set each one up so the SAB Miller logistics guys can just slot them seamlessly into the group's operations. This business is quite literally made for them.

At eight o'clock that evening, we're still going. And I desperately want a fag. So I get a pad of paper, and I say to Domenic:

'OK. You write on a piece of paper what you're prepared to pay, and I'll write on another piece of paper what we're prepared to accept. I'm going outside with Ian now to have a fag, and when we come back in, you'll have your number on that pad, and I'll have my number on the fag packet. Then we'll know where we stand.'

So I'm outside with Ian and I tell him we should write £130 million on my fag packet. He tells me I'm crazy, it's too much.

'You're just being greedy now,' he says. 'You don't want to be greedy at such a vital point in the negotiation.' These turned out to be wise words.

'Come on,' I urge him, 'we can always come down. Let's go for it.'

'No,' he says. 'I want you to go in at £120 million.'

We go back in; I show my fag packet with £120 million written on it. Domenic pushes the pad over the table. His figure is £125 million.

Ian's face feigns surprise. He knows that, inside, I'm fuming: I now know that we could have got more. But I hold it in, I deliberately keep my ego in check, and I say to Domenic:

'OK, you've done me. Tell you what: go halves with me. Meet me halfway. Then I've only lost two and a half million quid.'

I have my sad face on. I've lost. Domenic beams: he's won. He reaches across the table and we finally settle on £122.5 million. We go down to the Market Tavern in Shepherd Market. I wait outside and have another fag and when I go in, Domenic de Lorenzo is standing at the bar in his pinstripe suit, with a massive smile from ear to ear. I go up to him all hangdog.

'I can't believe it,' I say, shaking my head. 'I can't believe I lost two and a half million quid.'

He grins, slaps me on the back and it's over.

Inside of me, kept out well out of view, I knew we had won massively. I'd come into this in 2011 with a business valued at £10 million, with a plan to sell it for £50 million in five years. We'd just sold it for £122.5 million in four years. But one of the key things about negotiations (remember, we'd shaken hands on the deal but we had still to go through all the pressure of completion) before it was set in stone is always to let the other side feel like they've won. Who made the right call that evening? Ian Colletts. That sound head of his knew we needed to allow a last-minute victory for Domenic because in doing so we were creating a lever for ourselves to resist onerous covenants[31] and warranties. Had we driven Domenic to the highest price we could get, then like my friend Rolf Munding a few years ago with the silly mistake I'd made in spoofing over the price of a sandwich after buying Kozel from him, I think we would have given SAB cause to come at us for every warranty they could get.

---

31 A covenant is a promise by a signatory to a contract which pledges that something has been done, will be done, or will not be done.

Chapter Eleven

Aftermath

The day after that gruelling session in the SAB Miller headquarters in Mayfair, I was back at work in Greenwich. We'd shaken hands on the deal but we had nothing in writing yet and in fact we hadn't even appointed either a lawyer or an advisor. The very next day, I even entertained Ian Molson of the Canadian beer group Molson for a tour of the Meantime brewery; his visit had been arranged a few weeks back, and he was another senior global beer executive interested in this little London craft beer company.

Completing on the sale was an entirely new and complex proposition. For me, this was new territory and I had to learn on the hoof, keep my wits about me and seek the best advice. My father-in-law Ronnie played a blinder at this point, pointing out to me that we might be able to translate some of Meantime's historic financial losses into tax credits. He suggested this to me over a game of golf and when I went in the next day and put it to Gary Whitlie, he nodded and agreed. Ronnie's insight ended up covering almost the entire cost of our advisory teams.

We approached Kathryn Davies to help us pick our advisors. Kathryn was just retiring then and a very smart and experienced corporate lawyer and partner at Slaughter & May – she was another invaluable contact introduction from Creepy. She suggested we use DLA Piper as our legal team and Sapient as the corporate advisor and we set about writing the heads of terms[32] for the sale. Fraser Anderson and Peter Hansen of Sapient were superb throughout this phase of the sale. Meanwhile, Domenic and his team were doing the same their side, and our advisors would then lock heads to thrash out the final version. Meanwhile, even though we'd got an agreement on the price, we were still effectively in 'selling' mode. Sue Clark came to visit me several times and we went over all the Meantime systems, looking at how they could best be incorporated into SAB Miller's operating systems. I knew this wouldn't be too much of an issue because since arriving in 2011 I'd effectively restructured the business with that very aim in mind.

I'd been trying to clear up our position at The Old Brewery in Greenwich in the months leading up to the sale because I knew that our tenancy wasn't durable enough to be regarded as an asset in the transaction. In some ways, The Old Brewery had always been a bit of a vanity project, allowing Hooky to do some microbrewing experiments there and then showcasing new beers at the bar. But our lease wasn't strong and thankfully I was finally able to sell the pub to Young's while we were still negotiating the heads

---

32 A heads of terms document sets out in brief the outline elements of the proposed deal, as a precursor to the eventual signed contract or agreement.

of terms with SAB Miller, so we went into the final deal bargaining with a little more cash in the bank and just one secure pub asset, The Greenwich Union.

By 10 April, we had finally appointed both DLA Piper and Sapient and the meetings started growing rapidly, with ever-increasing numbers of SAB Miller figures coming to see us, talking to Hooky about brewing plans and summoning more and more financials from our finance director Bob Emms, who was an absolute star throughout this whole process. The due diligence process was fully under way, with a dataroom set up to share every last piece of information about our business with the purchasers. Our core team now was Gary, Ian, Bob, Paul and me. By 27 April, we'd drawn up a complete list from our side of 'disclosures', i.e. everything we were legally obliged as directors to make sure that SAB Miller were aware of. None of them turned out to be a dealbreaker or a price changer. Our fantastically efficient commercial lawyer at DLA Piper, Tim Wright, who with his assistant was pretty much camping out at the Blackwall Lane brewery and putting in the same kind of hours as me, interrogated every single one of us, demanding to know absolutely everything that could be considered a liability.

This was now a real pressure cooker situation, playing with extremely high stakes, and yet the only people at Meantime who knew were the board and our finance team led by Bob. Everyone else, all the way up to Mel and Rich, was completely in the dark: the business had to keep going as normal, just in case something unexpected happened and the deal fell through. Going into the first week of May, I was probably working 18 to 20 hours a day, operating completely on adrenaline, taking endless meetings with lawyers from both sides. Finally, on 8 May, both sides agreed on the wording of the sales purchase agreement (SPA), and we signed.

But it wasn't over yet. We then had to get 70 per cent of our shareholders to agree the deal; 70 per cent would then trigger the 'drag and tag' provisions of the company's shareholder agreement, obliging the remaining 30 per cent to agree, but ideally we needed to get 90 per cent. Hooky, Ben, Tony and I looked over our shareholder list, split them up between us, and then went out to speak to every one of them. Within two days, we had agreement from 92 per cent – we couldn't locate the others in time. This was a very emotional period: I gave the news to two of the original shareholders, both of whom had decided to step down as employees on my arrival, feeling probably correctly that they wouldn't enjoy my new management style, and the relief and joy from both was hugely gratifying. I will never forget seeing another shareholder literally break down in tears in front of me on hearing how much money he and his family were going to make. When I asked him why he was so emotional, he told me that he'd been made redundant from his banking job, he'd just been diagnosed with diabetes and he had two children needing funding through university: the deal came at just the right time. For Hooky and for Ben Joseph, it was a tremendous feeling I think to be able to go and see the people who had invested in them from the start, to give them the news that their investment had paid off, big time.

On the sale of Meantime, all our employed staff who had been with us for a minimum of six months received a share of the sale proceeds. We had put aside shares through our employee benefit trust (EBT) during the fundraise in 2011. I also bought some shares back from a company shareholder in 2014 and put them in the EBT. The proceeds were just shy of £1 million and were shared with the staff over 2015. It paid some large sums to long-standing loyal employees, and we also rewarded ten of the key employees (about 25 per cent) of the head office team with share options. The main key players all did very well. At the last share option issue in January 2015, the Meantime shares were valued at £7 a share. We sold for just under £40 a share so the profits were large and life changing for all who received them.

The pressure was immense during this whole period. Two weeks before the SPA was signed on 8 May, Bash, our formidable Albanian manager of the bottling line, came to see Hooky and told him that a crucial ball bearing keeping the whole line working was damaged. If we didn't get a replacement soon, the whole line could blow up. At the same time, we couldn't afford to stop bottling. So Hooky ordered a replacement from Germany, and the blooming thing took two weeks to arrive. Bash literally fitted that new ball bearing in on the morning of 8 May and we finally breathed a collective sigh of relief. Replacing the bottling line would have cost us a million pounds, which would have come off the sale price.

At last, we were able to tell the team. On the evening of Thursday 14 May, we told the senior managers and instructed them to tell their staff at nine the following morning that the business had been sold to SAB Miller. The press were informed at the same time. We then called a town hall at 3.30 pm on Friday 15 May. The pressure, the expectation, the sheer bloody effort of it all got to me, and as I stood up to address my colleagues, I began to feel my voice breaking, so much so that I had to stand back and let Hooky take over. It was emotional for all of us: everyone was part of a staff share option scheme so would benefit financially, and some long-standing members would become millionaires overnight.

When the news broke in the press, there was a lot of media noise. Most of the coverage was positive, particularly from the broadsheets who viewed it as a strong indicator of the strength of the British beer industry. One or two writers, however, writing either in the tabloids or in the trade press, chose to go down the knocking route, suggesting somehow that Hooky and I had 'sold out', that Meantime would suffer from joining forces with such a massive group as SAB. Hooky in particular took those slightly snide reports very personally, and I sympathised: of all the people in the world less likely to compromise over the quality of a pint of beer, that man would be Alastair Hook. He was remaining in charge of Meantime's brewing; it was the ownership of the company which had changed. But sadly it can sometimes be the case in our country that success attracts that kind of griping in the press; you never witness such negativity in a more business-positive country like the USA. But we were big boys, we had to live with it. I had always had a good relationship with the press over the four years at Meantime, with journalists like Simon Jack, the BBC's business reporter, going out of their way to give us fair coverage. So one or two people wanted to chew on sour grapes? Their problem, not mine.

One media outlet which remained consistently fair to us throughout my time at Meantime was the trade publication *Propel* edited by Paul Charity. Two months after the sale, Paul revealed that Hooky had been named Brewer of the

Year by the All-Party Parliamentary Beer Group. The piece read:

> As the founder of Meantime Brewing Company, Hook is most notably attributed as one of the true pioneers of the craft beer revolution in the UK. With humble beginnings in a small flat in Greenwich, Hook's decision to establish one of the UK's first modern craft breweries came in 2000 when he, and a group of like-minded friends, grew tired of the mass-market homogenisation of beers at the time. Andrew Griffiths, MP for Burton and Uttoxeter and chairman of the All-Party Parliamentary Beer Group, said: 'Alastair Hook is one of the most passionate and inspiring brewers not just in the UK, but in the world. One of the pioneers of Britain's thriving craft beer scene, Alastair's dedication and knowledge is second to none.'

That was a nice way to round off the sale period.

We had agreed with SAB Miller that the acquisition price would not be revealed for a year, and so everyone who was given the details of the deal, including our staff, was obliged to sign non-disclosures. It's a credit to everyone that the price did stay out of the press until SAB Miller themselves announced it in their annual report 12 months later. Until that time, the beer industry – the family brewers, the global group managers, the beer writers in the press, the stock researchers – all generally believed that we must have sold the company for somewhere between £50 and £60 million.

Those were certainly the figures that were speculated in the newspapers and the trade press. This was how the *Daily Telegraph* kicked off their story: 'SAB Miller, the global beer giant behind Peroni and Fosters, has targeted Britain's fast-growing craft beer scene by snapping up Meantime Brewing Company in a deal that could value the brewer at as much as £50 million.' You can imagine the reactions, then, when the actual figure was revealed a year later.

Throughout this mad, hectic period, Em was left to organise the renovation of the house we'd bought in Greenwich, the arrival of my brother and his family from Australia and our upcoming wedding on 3 July. I wasn't able to be of much help to her and she did an amazing job keeping everything going under these extraordinary circumstances. I'll never forget the day, of course, and one thing that still sticks in my mind and gives me a smile every time I think of it is the image of Hooky at our wedding, sitting outside Davy's wine bar in Greenwich wearing a Hawaiian shirt and with a big, happy grin on his face.

It's difficult to describe the deflation that comes with the successful conclusion of such an intense four years of close business comradeship. I know I wasn't alone among the Meantime team in feeling strangely low for many months following the sale; it was as though the adrenaline had all finally leaked out of me. On the night of the legal completion of the sale, Em took me to the West End to see the top show at the time, *The Book of Mormon* – I had to walk out at the interval because I couldn't even hear the words, my brain was so empty. I'd say it took me a good 18 months finally to get a perspective on what we'd all been through and I know I wasn't the only one who experienced that.

Oh, and I should mention too: all the Meantime shareholders, including me, actually received the funds from SAB Miller for their shares on 5 June 2015. It could have been any one of a number of dates in June in fact, but I expressly requested to Sue Clark and her team that the transfers be made on that day. The 5th of June was the date of my father's birthday. Point proven? I'm still trying to work it out.

Chapter Twelve

The Pint Test

'd hope that you can tell by now just how much I'm aware of the inspiration, guidance and education I've received over the years from a wide range of bosses, colleagues, business acquaintances and friends. I'm just sorry that I haven't been able to mention every one of them. A successful career really is about being aware of how much you're learning while in the meantime you're focusing on something else. If you're open to self-improvement, then you have a chance of achieving whatever ambitions you set for yourself.

I could pick out any number of people who have inspired me but there's one particular fellow who taught me a crucial thing about people. Barry Connolly is a very successful businessman, one of the most successful business people in Ireland. He has a wide range of business interests, from property through to energy bars, but I got to know him while I was running Miller Brands UK and he was the main distributor in Ireland for Miller beers. I described earlier what a merry dance he conducted during our negotiations with him when he was opposing Heineken. Barry once explained to me how he thought about people, and he called his process the Pint Test.

He described it as follows: if you have established that the person you're thinking about is someone you'd be happy going to have a pint with, you probably like them. That's the first important principle: try to work with people you like. Then you have to ask yourself, as you're sipping your pint and exchanging banter: do I respect this person? That's a different question. It's possible to like someone but not really respect them and if that's the case, you need to be careful. You can't spend your time in business with people that you like but don't respect. Finally, you must decide: do I trust this person? Once more, this is a different question. You can like someone, you can respect them, but if you've identified that you don't trust them, then in business and often in life, walk away.

Ever since Barry in his sincere way explained to me his Pint Test, I've tended to summarise people that way myself and I've found it a reliable indicator of whether you should be in business with someone. Most people who pass the Pint Test are like you: they want to give of their best, they want the best for you. They may beat you in a competition but they'll do it fairly. With one or two rare exceptions, all my colleagues at Meantime passed the Pint Test.

What's also illuminating is that the Pint Test applies equally to brands. The brands we all favour tend to be those we trust, respect and like; we apply the same methods for analysing brands as we do people. Once you realise that as a brand owner, it becomes much more obvious how you need to craft the complete product package you are offering to the consumer. Why on earth would anyone really be interested in building loyalty to a brand which failed the Pint Test?

Of course, we all went our various ways after Meantime. A period as intense as those four years between 2011 and 2015 will take its toll and most people felt the need to move on. I stayed on for a year, according to the terms of the sale agreement with SAB Miller, and in fact the following year, in 2016, I effectively sold Meantime for a second time: as I'd suspected it would, ABI announced its acquisition of SAB Miller, creating the biggest brewing conglomerate in the world, and ABI immediately set about selling the SAB Miller European assets, including Peroni and Meantime, to the Japanese beer giant Asahi, who own Meantime to this day. Once that sale was complete, my role was over and that's when Em and I started to investigate houses on the south coast; we'd both done enough time in London.

Hooky stayed on at Meantime and only resigned as a director at the end of 2019. He's still doing what he's always done best, brewing amazing beers. Others are doing well at rival craft beer brands like Camden and Two Tribes; some have used their sale proceeds to invest in new brewing or pub ventures. The Meantime years were so well documented and the sale so widely publicised that, for most of our staff, just the mere mention of having worked at Meantime would give them the edge in any recruitment process. A fair few of the employees elected to stay on at Meantime once it had been sold, first to SAB Miller and subsequently to Asahi, and some remain there, happy to be benefiting from life inside a major corporation. In particular, the sales and marketing team has flourished under corporate leadership, perhaps reflecting the fact that, as an ex-corporate myself, I had brought in more established working methods.

I don't see myself as an entrepreneur. I spent most of my career as a salaried employee of large organisations, and only the last few years as an entrepreneur/intrapreneur. These years have been successful for me largely because I've had the experience I had, I'd learned from it and I'd found a brand which had the latent, unexploited power to be able to respond to the assiduous application of tried and tested business rules. I'd contend that many successful business people who are referred to as entrepreneurs in fact do what I did: they apply lessons they've learned and they are absolutely single minded in doing so. I wasn't a brewer; Hooky was the brewer. I wasn't a creative; Ian Cassie was our creative. I wasn't a brand manager; Rich stepped up to the mark and delivered that role in spades. I wasn't a financial controller; Gary Whitlie and Ian Colletts, as trained chartered accountants, kept an eye on Bob Emms and Paul Robinson as we ran Meantime's finances with a firm hand. If I wasn't any of those things, what was I? It's essentially a question of leadership: Meantime was a fantastic business that wasn't delivering on its potential, and it needed someone – who turned out to be me – to step in and gather together all the elements that would be required to transform it into a leading national brand. I'm not saying anyone could have done it; you had to have gone through what I'd gone through the previous 25 years to gather together the experience to be match ready. Therefore my role was primarily that of leadership, leading by example and leading by system, allowing everyone to perform as well as they were able within a clearly managed sales and marketing strategy.

From an early age, I knew that, somehow, I'd do all right; I'd be able to stand on my own two feet and at some point

I'd make a few bob. From my first proper job managing that little Barratts shoe shop in Darlington to taking over as chief executive at Meantime, I always applied pretty clear rules for myself:

- **Never be a slacker.** Results only arise from the application of energy and all successful business people are relentless in that way.

- **Don't accept how others categorise you.** (But do listen to what they say about you.) Most people, including good managers, can't see beyond what you currently are, and therefore categorise you in a static fashion. You need to hold on to your vision of what you could be. Take heed of what your managers say about you. While they may not always see your potential, a good manager will always tell you where you need to improve.

- **Listen more than you speak.** Apply the rule of two ears, two eyes and one mouth: use them in that order.

- **Manage your own career.** If you're just starting out, then do your best to plot your course so that you get promoted into jobs that will increase your knowledge, skills and experience. Don't be driven by money or job title.

- **Do something you love doing.** It's not always about the money – sometimes the rewards follow your instinct.

- **Be honest about yourself and with other people.** If you've got an itch, scratch it: I was always conscious of having flunked my education so by getting an MBA

I could prove to myself that I was as good as anyone else. I love the ethos quoted to me by a Liverpudlian once: no one's better than me, and I'm not better than anyone else. Over time, too, I learned to be honest in my own self-appraisals about my motivation, and realised it wasn't as simple as just wanting to succeed; I also needed to prove to the father I never knew that I could get somewhere without him.

🍾 **Be self-aware and self-critical, and understand your own risk profile relative to your capabilities.** When I was in my mid-thirties, with a young family and a big mortgage, my appetite for risk was quite low and therefore a salaried corporate job suited me. By the time I was in my mid-forties, my marriage was failing and my kids were in a much stronger position; I was ready then to embrace the risk of diving into Meantime. Now I'm in my mid-fifties and I've experienced the roller coaster thrill of the Meantime adventure and reaped the financial benefits from it, I know my risk appetite has reduced again.

🍾 **Always apply the Pint Test.** Don't just be satisfied by liking people. Check whether you both respect and trust them as well.

All the above helped me make my own luck and maybe might help you make yours. They seemed to work for me. As I said when I started out on this book, if you're thinking of building your own consumer brand, then I hope some of this might have been of use. If we happen to bump into each other in a pub one of these days, I hope I pass your Pint Test.

Appendix

The Brewer's Art

As you've discovered from reading this book, while I've never lost my taste for beer and my love of the industry, I can never claim to have anything like the brewer's art. That's a specialism that only a few, talented people I've been fortunate enough to know can claim as their own. But I particularly relish the process of brewing, because in many ways the patience, diligence, energy and application which go into making a fabulous beer reflect the qualities I believe you'll need to achieve success. Let's end, then, with a nod to the world's great brewers and, I know it's sentimental, but I think it would be remiss of me not to describe how this fine product, which has been central to my career, is made.

Malting

Before the brewer begins to work his or her magic at the brewery, they must acquire the malted hops they need to begin the brewing process. Barley is the cereal best suited for beer, a choice confirmed by hundreds of years of brewing all over the world. But it must first be treated to release the enzymes which can break down the starch in the grain into sugar. This is known as malting, in which the barley grains are steeped in water for a couple of days and then laid out on a flat surface to allow them to begin to germinate. Once germination has begun, it is brought to a halt through the heating of the grains in drying kilns. The brewmaster who has ordered the malted hops from the specialist maltster will always specify the type of product required: extra heat in the kiln, for example, will result in a darker malt which will add colour and flavour to the finished beer. Once completed, the finished malt is despatched to the brewer.

Milling

The first task for the brewer is the milling or crushing of the malted barley grains into what is known as 'grist' – hence the phrase, 'all grist to the mill'. The grist is essentially fragmented malted barley grains whose centre is now accessible to water, which will be added to it at the next stage.

Mashing

The brewer now mixes the milled malt with hot water in a process known as mashing. This is normally done in a big container called a mash tun, with about three parts of water to one part of malt. There are traditionally two methods of mashing: the typical British technique of holding the hot water at a consistent temperature, and the specialist German brewing technique of holding the mash at varying temperatures in a stepped process achieved by regularly removing the mash to heat it and then returning it to the tun to achieve a higher heat. The objective of the mashing process is to encourage the natural enzymes in the malt to convert the starch into maltose and dextrose, both forms of sugar. It is the maltose which converts into alcohol while the dextrose remains as sugar to add flavour. The resulting sugar-heavy liquid is known as the wort.

Lautering

The mash is now pumped from the mash tun into a lauter tun and is gently recirculated to ensure that unwanted debris and proteins can be filtered out of the liquid wort. Once the liquid is clean, the brewer allows it to run off into the kettle, leaving the grain bed at the bottom. This bed is sprayed with hot water to rinse out any sugars which have been trapped in the grain, a process known as sparging. The end of this stage, the lautering stage, leaves a clean, sweet liquid wort to go on to the next step, and a pile of spent grain which is sent to the country for farmers to use as animal feed.

The boil

The wort is now boiled in a big brew kettle and the chemical reactions which take place during the boiling sterilise it. Hops are added to the wort during the boiling process and, depending on what stage the brewer introduces the hops, the resulting liquid will be more bitter or less so, more aromatic or less so. Here again we see the art and the creativity in the brewer's application of the science.

Whirlpool

Once the wort has been boiled and the hops have been added, the liquid then passes into a whirlpool where the dense proteins and vegetable matter from the hops, known as the trub, are separated from the liquid. The effect of the whirlpool is to throw the pure liquid to the sides and collect the trub in the centre of the tank, making it easier to gather off the clear liquid wort from the sides.

Cooling

The hot wort, once it has been separated from the trub during the whirlpool process, now needs to be cooled rapidly in order to avoid damage from oxidation. The speed of cooling is also influenced by the need to stop the production of dimethyl sulphide, which the wort can produce if allowed to stay warm for too long and will give the beer a poor taste. Cooling takes place in a vessel provided with a plate heat exchanger.

Fermentation

The brewer's alchemical magic really becomes apparent with the addition of yeast to the wort. This fermentation process usually takes place in large cylindrical vessels with a conical foundation, which allows the yeast to sink to the bottom while it is eating into the sugar in the wort, creating more yeast until the fermentation point is reached; at this point there is no oxygen left and the yeast begins to make alcohol and carbon dioxide. This slow, cold fermentation is what produces the hop and malt flavours of craft beers because the yeast, by dropping to the bottom of the tank, doesn't impose its flavour so strongly. With traditional ales, the warmer and faster process enables the yeast to rise to the top of the tank, thereby creating more of a yeasty taste that we expect from an ale.

Maturation

Once primary fermentation has taken place, the beer is held in a tank at a very low temperature for a period of time to mature and develop in flavour. Lagers are matured for eight weeks or more at freezing temperatures to allow flavours and aromas to emerge and to strip away sulphur compounds. When maturation times are cut (which cost-cutting accountants at big groups can sometimes try and impose), the quality of the finished product declines.

Acknowledgements

This book (as I suspect many others were) was the result of the Covid lockdown and pandemic. It gave me some time to collect my thoughts and start recording them. What came out was this book.

Over the years I have been encouraged by several people to record my memoir with particular emphasis on the Peroni and Meantime stories. With the world locked up and few things to distract me, I finally took on the challenge.

I wished to achieve three things when writing this book:

1. share my journey and learnings

2. record the strategic foundations upon which the Peroni and Meantime successes were based

3. recognise and thank the people I have had the pleasure to meet or work with. They undoubtedly influenced and helped me on my journey. Many are mentioned by name in the book. Thank you.

Unfortunately there are many that I couldn't include in this text so please indulge me while I reel off a few names. Some taught me good lessons which I followed, some others which I did not. Maybe if I write another book I can expand on this…

Here goes:

Thank you to those who inspired me to write this business memoir – my lovely wife Ems, Dom, Leo, Ed and last but not least Simon Petherick who tried to teach me how to do it.

Those who have been kind enough to proofread it and ensure it is a fair reflection of me: Ems (several times), Fenners, Mark Ross, Lambo (my mother-in-law – I've got a very good one!), Benji P the javelin thrower, Dan Mahoney 'the brief', Mum, Annie, Sam, George, Alice and Izzy.

A big thank you also to Justin, Ian and Keith, who have been so generous with their reviews.

Thank you also to people who I didn't get the chance to mention, a few more special ones as follows: Jonathan Webster, Peter Furness Smith (the Vicar), the Robbos and Lees Jones clans, Rooney Anand, Bev Hubbard, Jonathan Duck, Ray Yarwood, Ted Tuppen, Ivan Walpole, Willie Donnelly, Jay Maling, Dave McKenzie, Al Kemp, David Ellis, Robert Humphries, Dr Harry White, John Finney, the Dawks clan, Mark and Ang Collins, Noddy Nerdrum (my MBA mentor), Phil Ley, Tony Hughes, Adam Martin, Simon Treanor (a top bloke to work with in a team), Dave Halliday (aka Shonks), Tim and Phil (my old school muckers along with Fenners) – and all the 'Meantimers' who haven't been mentioned in this book.

References

Bowman, C. & Faulkner, D. (1996) *Competitive and Corporate Strategy*. Irwin Professional Publishing.

Brooks, A.W. & John, L.K. (2018) 'The Surprising Power of Questions'. *Harvard Business Review*, May–June 2018.

Carnegie, D. (2006) *How To Win Friends And Influence People*. Vermilion.

Johnson, G., Scholes, K. & Whittington, R. (2007) *Exploring Corporate Strategy*. Financial Times/Prentice Hall. 8th edition.

Kahneman, D. & Tversky, A. (1979) 'Prospect theory: an analysis of decision under risk'. *Econometrica* 47(2).

Kotter, J. (2012) *Leading Change*. Harvard Business Review Press.

Porter, M.E. (2004) *Competitive Strategy*. Free Press.

Welch, J. (2005) *Winning*. HarperCollins.